Erotic Revolutionaries

Black Women, Sexuality, and Popular Culture

Shayne Lee

Hamilton Books
A member of
The Rowman & Littlefield Publishing Group
Lanham • Boulder • New York • Toronto • Plymouth, UK

Copyright © 2010 by
Hamilton Books
4501 Forbes Boulevard
Suite 200
Lanham, Maryland 20706
Hamilton Books Acquisitions Department (301) 459-3366

Estover Road
Plymouth PL6 7PY
United Kingdom

Library of Congress Control Number: 2010927841
ISBN: 978-0-7618-5228-5 (paperback : alk. paper)
eISBN: 978-0-7618-5229-2

Contents

Acknowledgments

I owe a debt of gratitude to many people. Angela Davis and Susan Douglas for enlightening me to the fact that popular culture is a valuable site for feminist empowerment and subversive sexual politics. Camille Paglia, Maria Elena Buszek, Jessica Valenti, Rebecca Walker, and Jane Gallop for exhibiting sexy brands of feminism that inform every page of this book. Mimi Schippers for allowing me to become a student again by auditing her wonderful course on sexuality studies. Carol Ross and Martha Pitts for reading earlier drafts and catching embarrassing mistakes. Ananda Leeke for her listening ear and invaluable input on Gen X black sexuality. Travis Lee deserves special recognition for leaving his mark on every chapter with trenchant observations and thoughtful suggestions. Most importantly, I thank the erotic revolutionaries of popular culture who wage a relentless war against the politics of respectability and gendered double standards. These pagan goddesses inspire millions of women to be more sexually proactive and empowered.

Introduction:
Erotic Revolutionaries
of Black Sexuality

Conservative sexual behavior is the foundation of the performance of middle-class black womanhood.

—Lisa Thompson

We need to learn that bodily pleasure belongs to us; it is our birthright.

—Rebecca Walker

As I write this introduction, I am teaching a course called "African-American Feminist Thought." Our class has a diverse mix of women (along with three men) from multiple ethnic and socioeconomic backgrounds. As provocateur and gadfly, I enjoy starting fiery discussions, and sex is often my trusty accelerant. For example, I begin one class with a thought experiment asking my students if they would accept a sexual proposition to secure their dream job. While my three male students say yes without hesitation, the women are split. Some express sentiments like, "I've slept with boys I didn't really like before, so why not get something great out of it," and "What's the big deal, it's just sex?" Others insist they would never compromise their integrity for employment. Twenty minutes into the exchange, Emma-Caitlin calls our attention to a consistent pattern: most of the women rejecting the sexual proposition are black; none of the women accepting the proposition are black. Her observation unwittingly shifts us toward a new topic: black women and sexual repression.

Valerie references the autobiography of the late basketball legend Wilt Chamberlain where he claims that white women have fewer sexual hang-ups than black women. Christina mentions the brash comic Mo'Nique as the only black woman to discuss masturbation in the public forum. My students detonate theories on everything from why black football players have "night-time integration" with white coeds to why sexual reticence actually makes black teens more susceptible to pregnancy. The class session dwindling, I open the floor for final thoughts concerning the impetus behind black women's alleged sexual repression. Seizing the last word, Marilyn contends that such erotic reservations function as black women's defense mechanisms against centuries of rape, sexual stereotyping, and harassment in America.

Gwendolyn Pough's student offers a similar assessment in a women's studies course when she reproves female rappers like Lil' Kim and Foxy Brown for flaunting their sexuality against the backdrop of the systemic sexual oppression black women have endured in the United States for centuries (2004). Pough believes her student's condemnation exemplifies the manner in which black women learn to think conservatively about sexuality and scrupulously supervise their representation to avoid participating in the historical legacy of sexual stereotyping and exploitation.

In Mya Baker's documentary, *Silence: In Search of Black Female Sexuality in America,* cultural theorist Tricia Rose confirms that a long-standing practice of sexual abuse during slavery and beyond convinces many black women that acting as sexual subjects presupposes the enduring of shame and public embarrassment, hence the choice by an overwhelming contingency of black women to downplay their viability as sexual subjects. In the same documentary, gynecologist and sex expert Hilda Hutcherson reveals how the residual effect of growing up in a sexually silent and over-protective environment begets the demise of her first marriage:

> I could not share my sexuality or feelings of sex with my partner because I had suppressed them because of my upbringing. I could not open up and enjoy sex with the one person in the room that I loved. And I regret that and I resent that. So many years of my life that should have been pleasurable were not. And though I've forgiven those people, it still hurts, and it's still inside me.

Other interviewees discuss growing up in black families and engaging social networks that rarely broach the topic of sex, except to offer pithy exhortations for women to "keep their panties up, dresses down, and legs closed" to avoid getting pregnant or contracting a sexually transmitted disease.

The above discussions reveal how African-American women's quest for societal propriety leads many to assume a particular kind of sexual saintliness that Evelyn Higginbotham (1992) identifies as the "politics of respectability" in which black women suppress or deny erotic expression and advise those around them to do the same. With overt attempts to downplay sexuality, black women resist negative images and sexual stereotypes in an attempt to secure respectability and empowerment for all black Americans (Hammonds 1999). Candice Jenkins confirms that many black women respond to sexual oppression by attempting to regulate their behavior "in the service of creating an inviolable respectability" (2007: 12). Put simply, the politics of respectability is prevalent in nineteenth-century black feminist thought and influences black women to accept sexual chastity for the greater good of social responsibility. Such sexual sanctimony has roots in slavery, when slave masters consigned black women to the position of slave breeders and objects for sexual gratification; in response to such oppressive conditions, black women learned to de-emphasize their sexuality. Rennie Simson (1983) cites examples of this phenomenon in the form of autobiographies by former female slaves whose experiences with sexual abuse led them to negate their sexuality in later years, thus validating the contention that slavery instituted a momentous assault on black sexual identity (Davis 1981; Battle and Barnes 2009).

Exploring the intersection between race, ethnicity, and sexuality, Joane Nagel (2003) demonstrates how African Americans' sexual history in the United States is intimately connected with organized systems of social oppression. She writes:

> The roots of contemporary racism and racial conflict were planted early in American history in sexual soil, they were fed by sexual fears and desires, and they thrived in an environment of lust, greed, and demeaning sexual stereotypes. To understand contemporary U.S. race relations it is important to understand the role of sexuality in building and supporting racial boundaries. Sexuality, in particular the sexual exploitation of slaves with its associated intensities of appetite, shame, and denial, was and remains a vital part of the U.S. racial order. (125)

Nagel presents sex as an interior component of race and ethnicity, with race and ethnicity, in return, as core features of sexual and moral schemes. Such arrangements and boundaries, particularly concerning African-American female sexuality and its historical legacy of exploitation, create sexual expectations that construct and define sexual identities, desires, and practices. These interconnections suggest that past social relations of exploitation affect current sexual preferences and practices. Nagel provides theoretical insight for understanding how Higginbotham's idea of the politics of respectability emerges from slavery as a main staple in black female sexual presentation and performance.

Several scholars elucidate how the politics of respectability takes new form in the early twentieth-century. Hazel Carby (1999) argues that when African-American women migrate to cities, new problems emerge that middle-class blacks perceive as threats to black progress; problems that are expressed in "fears of a rampant and uncontrolled female sexuality; fears of miscegenation; and fears of the assertion of an independent black female desire that has been unleashed through migration" (29). Carby contends that this moral panic, marinated in the bourgeois ideology of the Jazz Age, incites a contingency of churches, organizations, and lodging houses, as well as the National Association of Colored women's clubs and similar organizations nationwide to synchronize efforts toward protecting black women from sexual vices and what they perceive to be the trappings of city life.

Similarly, Candice Jenkins (2007) discusses how the early twentieth-century black women's club movement works feverishly to recover black women's sexuality from disgrace by demonstrating decorum and family stability and encouraging other black women to emulate bourgeois values, "the very same Victorian values that had been used to exclude black people from ideals of kinship and sexuality" (12). Hence, the late nineteenth century and early twentieth century beget a surge of coordinated attempts to pressurize African-American women to downplay their sexuality as an antidote to the sexual exploitation and objectification inflicted upon them.

Lisa Thompson (2009) also exposes how a correlation between the politics of respectability and the development of black middle-class female sexual ideals suppress the sexual performance of black women. Thompson explains how the "black lady" persona emerges as an archetype in conjunction with social codes and proprietary morals of twentieth-century reformers who maneuver on behalf of more humane treatment of African Americans. Social pressure on the African-American woman to conduct herself like a "black lady" incorporates a meticulous management of sexual representation, relying "heavily upon aggressive shielding of the body; concealing sexuality; and foregrounding morality, intelligence, and civility as a way to counter negative stereotypes" (Thompson 2009: 2). Yearning to portray blacks positively, novelists and playwrights project literary and cultural delineations of middle-class black women as intensely uncorrupted and morally upstanding.

Other works discuss how the devaluation and sexual exploitation of black women during slavery and beyond impact contemporary sexual politics (hooks 1981; Hine 1989; Higginbotham 1992; Hammonds 1994; 1999; James 1999; Battle and Barnes 2009). Through rigid self-surveillance and careful policing of each other's bodies, many black women continue to hold each other accountable to middle-class sexual decorum. The largest national sexuality study since the acclaimed mid-twentieth-century Kinsey Reports reveals that African-American women are considerably less likely to masturbate, use a vibrator, enjoy and achieve orgasm through masturbation, give and receive oral sex, and enjoy giving and receiving oral sex than other women (Laumann et al. 2000). Similarly, two prominent studies on black sexuality suggest that black women appear to be more sexually conservative, less knowledgeable about sexual anatomy, less probable to engage in oral sex, and not as likely to initiate intercourse with their partners as white women (Wyatt 1997; Staples 2006).

The politics of respectability, though originating for the protection of black women, acts as an apparatus of social control and gender inequality. In this way, society polices women "into silence about sex, socially constructed modesty, and self-regulating repression of behavior and fantasy" (Johnson 2002a: 1). The image of a bourgeois sexually reticent "black lady" may seem to be a temporary reprieve in lieu of other more historically charged stereotypes, but she is an equally undignified appendage to the enumeration of black female misrepresentation (Thompson 2009). Women's evasiveness toward sexual stimulation represents an unambiguous variance between the physical experience of sex and the social forces that delineate and confine sexual experience (Schwartz and Rutter 1998), or as Leonore Tiefer puts it, "Censorship harms women because women need sexual empowerment, not sexual protection" (1995: 134).

Scholars are quick to calculate the effects of a politics of respectability as an instrument of regulatory regimes in the everyday lives of black women, but are slow to appraise how it influences black feminist scholarship, which has yet to generate a discursive attack against middle-class systems of sexual regulation that monitor black female sexuality. Academic works on black sexual politics have yet to produce a discourse on sex and sexuality that celebrates the erotic theatricality of the sexual female body. For example, the new anthology *Black Sexualities: Probing Powers, Passions, Practices, and Policies* (2009) covers a myriad of topics on black sexuality including the black transgender experience, racial justice and HIV disclosure, black masculinity in hip-hop, sexuality and families, etc. but does not offer one article overtly advocating black female sexual agency. While one article acknowledges that black scholars often approach black sexuality as pathological (McGruder 2009), no article challenges the politics of respectability. The one article that addresses black female sex workers exposes the psychological and physical costs of sex work, while overlooking the potential for black female sex workers to offer empowering models for black female sexuality (Tatum 2009). The groundbreaking anthology's failure to include articles on black female sexual agency speaks volumes about the current state of black sexual politics and black feminist thought in academia.

While feminist scholars from other racial and ethnic backgrounds explore new and empowering visions for female sexual exploration, black academics continue to show little interest in deploying sexuality as a strategy of power. More humorously put, feminists writing about sexuality generally give you the critique or the clit (Johnson 2002a). Black academics, however, mostly offer the critique. Hence, as Evelynn Hammonds suggests, "We know more about the elision of sexuality by black women than we do about the possible varieties of expression of desire" (1994: 143).

One must step outside the corridors of academia to find black women pursuing bodily pleasure with a sense of entitlement, or celebrating sexualized women as assertive and strong. Prominent pro-sex works invariably arrive from black feminists outside of the academy like Audre Lorde and Jewelle Gomez (and their intellectual successors Rebecca Walker and Tara Roberts), while black feminist scholarship is virtually devoid of sex-positive classic texts. Regarding sexualized female bodies, black academics consume themselves with detecting patriarchy up to its old tricks again, attentively unearthing oppression but seldom advocating agency, autonomy, and pleasure. While black feminist scholars patrol the airways for degrading images of women, African-American women in popular culture recommence a legacy of insubordination against the politics of respectability.

Blues singers like Bessie Smith and Gertrude "Ma" Rainey, dancers like Katherine Dunham and Josephine Baker, pop divas like Tina Turner and Grace Jones, and movie stars like Dorothy Dandridge and Pam Grier explode the bourgeois decorum of their eras and negotiate new frontiers for female sensuality. More recently, imaginative poets Jessica Holter and Ursula Rucker tantalize audiences with erotic communication; artist Mickalene Thomas creates evocative paintings on black female beauty and sexual power; choreographer Jawole Willa Jo Zollar elevates the theme of "erotic integrity" in the recent performances of her Urban Bush Women modern dance company; rappers Missy Elliot, Lil' Kim, and Trina present sex and sexiness as empowering and fun; soulful singer Me' Shell Ndegeocello creates new spaces for evocative same-sex eroticism in her lyrics; video vixens Melyssa Ford and Karrine Steffans radiate the sexuality of pagan goddesses; and black female characters Tracy "Bird" Van Adams and Lynn Searcy display sexual vibrancy on television shows like *Soul Food* and *Girlfriends*. Without picking up a textbook, we can experience subversive sexual politics by watching pop cultural divas deconstruct conventional borders of female sexuality.

Michele Wallace (1990) asserts that lurking in the rear of feminist treatment of negative black media images is an essentialist notion of the "authentically black" woman who, steadfast to bourgeois sensibilities, knows intrinsically how to uplift the race. Wallace's assertion rings true today. When feminist scholars traditionally approach black sexuality in popular culture, they show how media images oppress and misrepresent, paying little attention to the profound ways some pop cultural representations empower. Lisa Thompson indicates that such a narrow focus "leaves little room for black female empowerment through sexual representation or for subversive representational strategies presented for a black female spectator" (2009: 9).

Reversing this protectionist trend, Tricia Rose (1994), Angela Davis (1999), Hazel Carby (1999), Mark Anthony Neal (2003), and Lisa Thompson (2009) show how black women in popular culture also offer prescriptive models of sexual power and agency. Rose reveals how female rappers' displays of sexual freedom correlate with larger feminist narratives that subvert traditional perceptions of female sexuality and pleasure. Davis and Carby analyze the sexual politics of classical blues women who exhibit power and control over sexuality and defy the politics of respectability with lyrics and deeds. Neal explains why a pop singer's provocative allusion to self-pleasure is a "powerful articulation of self-defined black female sexuality" (2003: 68), and shows how a neo-soul singer raises the consciousness of black sexual politics with lyrics that challenge heterosexist perceptions of black identity. Thompson discloses how late-twentieth-century literary and dramatic texts represent a distinctive moment where black middle-class women in popular culture subvert bourgeois sensibilities. While the above works take important steps toward excavating popular culture for proactive visions of black female sexuality, this current work strives toward a more deliberately prescriptive sex-positive trajectory for black feminist thought and black sexual politics.

Erotic Revolutionaries: Black Women, Sexuality, and Popular Culture slides into intriguing new spaces where female sexual agency and black popular culture collide. This study presupposes that popular culture is an interesting terrain to see sexuality in ways that both confirm and subvert gendered arrangements of social power in society. Whereas many feminist writings focus their attention on how media representations of sexualized African-American women are problematic (hooks 1992; 1996; Bobo 1995; Collins 2004; Sharpley-Whiting 2007), this book reveals how many of the same representations offer nuggets of empowerment. Rather than depicting contemporary black female performers and sex symbols as exploited replications of nineteenth-century racism (hooks 1992; Collins 2004), I present them as feminists asserting discourses of sexual agency and autonomy through song, comedy, literature, personal narrative, sexual instruction, and presentation of selves in their art and everyday lives.

Chapter 1 opens the study with theoretical groundwork for my approach to sexuality from the analytic framework of sociology. Rather than embarking sexuality as an objective force or a biological reality independent of human experience, sociologists treat sexuality and the erotic as contingent upon humans interacting with codes that inform and guide various kinds of sexual interactions. I join a growing cohort of sociologists who use the "sexual script" as a metaphor suggesting the link between sexual performance and cultural modes of interpretation.

Scripting theorists assume that all sexual interactions depend on cognitive schemas to make sense of the encounter and frame possible actions and responses. Scripting theory gives credence to the creative ways that individual agents respond to, negotiate, and on occasion subvert structures for gender arrangements and sexual stratification. I contend that such a heuristic model is useful for exploring how black women in popular culture deploy discursive strategies that endorse female sexual agency and empowerment. I extract and apply rudiments from scripting theory, third wave feminism, popular culture, and black sexual politics to reveal the ways in which certain ideas, practices, norms, or "scripts" sustain hegemonic structures, and how subversive narratives can supplant those structures. While employing scripting theory, I diverge from most social constructionist studies of sexuality by treating cultural production and sexual politics as strategic locations of feminist struggle, and more acutely, by offering a prescriptive corrective for black sexual politics.

I deem my subjects erotic revolutionaries because they effectively wage war against the politics of respectability and challenge traditional scripts that offer men greater space to indulge in a fuller range of sexual expressivities. Some of my subjects bask in the ecstasies and mysteries of sexual desire; others create safe spaces for sexual discourse and confront patriarchal myths. All of my subjects are prototypes of what I call the new feminist chic: strong, smart, edgy, ambitious, socially-conscious, independent women who implicitly and explicitly encourage new generations toward sexual agency, exploration, and empowerment.

Chapter 2 studies how Janet Jackson, Beyoncé Knowles, and Jill Scott offer proactive scripts for women to respond to the vagaries and challenges of their love lives. They are award-winning vocalists and songwriters who fashion female personas encompassing a contingent of polarities: lustful and contemplative, aggressive and passive, seductive and seduced, vanquisher and victim, sexually satisfied and neglected, powerful and weak. They sometimes envision sexuality as an explosive force that brings much comfort, excitement, and exuberance; other times present sexuality as a destructive power that ruins relationships, keeps women up all night, makes them bitter, jealous, and abused. In their songs they take on various personas that demand sexual pleasure and warn men that uninspired sexual performance is not acceptable. Janet, Beyoncé, and Jill relish their own erotic power and portray women as complex sexual subjects.

Chapter 3 takes a revisionist look at Karrine Steffans' best-selling memoir *Confessions of a Video Vixen* and her ensuing vocation as a feminist provocateur raging against the regimes of patriarchal sexual discourse. Her memoir offers a sizzling account of a tumultuous time in her life and inadvertently piques a new curiosity in some women about what it is like to enjoy an adventurous sex life. Conversely, the destructive and humiliating aspects of her story lead others to suppose that sexual abstinence is the wiser course. Accordingly, while Karrine's poignant testimonies spark divergent opinions about female sexuality, pleasure, and vulnerability, they are nevertheless noteworthy for carving new space for such discourse. Her memoir, subsequent books, and concomitant career as a feminist agitator do much to deconstruct gendered double standards about sex, valorize female sexual agency, arouse new visions of sexual artistry, and guide countless women on a more proactive path toward self-transcendence.

Zane's novels feature powerful female protagonists who take risks, initiate sexual encounters, and judge men for bad performances. Thousands of women each year write letters and emails to Zane conveying how her stories revolutionize their sex lives by expanding their imaginations, expectations, and sexual repertoires. Chapter 4 explores the major themes in Zane's fictional worlds of unrestrained women who brag about lusting after male genitalia, share masturbatory techniques with friends, are proficient with a dizzying number of sex toys, and present a more complex vision of African-American women as sexually adventurous and proactive. Her female protagonists have healthy sexual appetites, and on some occasions, enact revenge on unfaithful partners by initiating their own affairs. Zane's fiction enlightens a woman to the belief that sex is like art, and that masterpieces may be wrought through detail, diligence, and creativity.

Chapter 5 discusses how sex experts like LaDawn Black and Hilda Hutcherson help women raise their sexual IQ and pursue new ways to attain sexual pleasure. Their books and videos encourage women to know and love their bodies and to explore new perspectives and information on numerous aspects of their sexuality and sexual experience. As one of the newest sexperts on the scene, Alexyss Tylor conjures up an entirely new genre: the comedic Internet morality play. Whether she is saluting her vagina or depicting wedding rings as male "nut brackets," her irascible YouTube clips will no doubt make women laugh while they learn about the intricacies of male and female relationships and the trappings of male sexual anatomy.

Chapter 6 explores how the tennis superstar, fashion designer, actress, and model Serena Williams transcends simple formulas concerning what is good for women and what objectifies them. Serena's complexities befuddle some traditional feminists because she is both strong yet girlie; competitively aggressive yet conventionally old-fashioned; sexy and sensual yet religious and demure. She is the poster child for Joan Morgan's third wave brand of feminism that is bold enough to "fuck with the grays" (1999: 59). She is equal parts power chick and pin-up girl and embraces no mandate of mutual exclusivity between such personas. Serena basks in a varying array of options and celebrates her individuality as a complex sexual subject.

The Reverend Susan Newman writes the book *OH GOD!: A Black Woman's Guide to Sex and Spirituality* because "somebody has to own up to the fact that black folks need to start talking about sex from the sphere of the church" (2002: 2). She sparks Christians to engage in evenhanded and straightforward dialogues with themselves and God about sex. She chides pastors for relegating sexual education to a simple prescription for women to abstain from pre-marital sex, which socializes women to fear sexual perspicuity. Instead, she argues that God-fearing women should be able to express themselves fully as sexual beings without guilt or shame. Unlike the conservative teachings of many black preachers, you won't find a single sentence in Susan Newman's book that lists abstinence amongst unmarried women's moral responsibilities. Chapter 7 reveals how Susan Newman and her conservative clerical counterparts Juanita Bynum and Ty Adams make the pulpit safe space for sexual discourse.

Television shows like *Def Comedy Jam* and *Comic View*, a movie like *The Queens of Comedy,* and comic venues in cities nationwide offer African-American women strategic opportunities to engage in explicit sexual discourse before large audiences. Chapter 8 explores how the comic stage gives Wanda Sykes, Sheryl Underwood, Mo'Nique, and other black female comics license to objectify men, debunk sexual stereotypes against women, air dirty laundry about deficient male sexual performance, vent frustrations about their own changing bodies, affirm their preference for younger men (and women) as sex partners, desensitize black audiences to taboo topics like oral sex, and discuss raunchy sexcapades while pronouncing to the world black women's inalienable status as sexually charged beings. Black female comics engage in the most erotic forms of public discourse and flip the script by converting men into the reluctant subjects of sexual scrutiny.

Tyra Banks' eroticism exudes through her sexualized actions and the topics she explores as host and controlling executive of her syndicated daytime television program *The Tyra Banks Show* as unmistakably as sensuality pervades her catwalks, rousing cameos in music videos, romantic liaisons with powerful men, and inclusion in *People* magazine's "50 Most Beautiful List." Chapter 9 is based on a three-year study of *The Tyra Banks Show* and delineates how Tyra engages celebrity guests, porn stars, prostitutes, and even politicians in confabs about their sex lives, and encourages women to accentuate their sexual power while maintaining a healthy dose of self-acceptance. Tyra puts on form-fitting dresses accentuating her curves and low necklines parading her ample endowment, often themselves the topic of discussion and exploration. She is trendy, stylish, and seductive, and loves to chat about sex, romance, and dating. She uses her popular talk show and her body as erotic terrain for women to engage in sexual discourse and bask in sensual energy.

Erotic Revolutionaries fuses scripting theory with pop cultural analysis and third wave feminism as weaponry in the feminist arsenal to fire the deathblow to the politics of respectability, an apparatus of sexual regulation against black female sexuality. This work rests on the premise that black women should have more safe spaces to engage a fuller range of sexual subjectivity, as men do, without reprisal. The book aims to loosen the politics of respectability's stranglehold on black feminist scholarship and awaken African-American academic counterparts to Jane Gallup, Joanna Frueh, Leslie Heywood, Maria Elena Buszek, and numerous other scholars who navigate wider spaces concerning pro-sexual visions of feminism and female sexual empowerment. Rather than consigning my subjects to the trite "Jezebel" hyper-sexualized archetype, I envision them as a creative band of feminists who carve out creative spaces for female sexual subjectivity.

Ken Plummer claims "there is little humping and pumping, sweatiness or sexiness in much sociological work" (2007: 24). *Erotic Revolutionaries* seeks to inject a little humping and pumping into sociological analysis, ultimately restoring the proverbial "clit" to its rightful place in black sexual politics. This book considers the ways in which a pro-sex vision can supplement the feminist quest for social and sexual equity by delving into popular culture to see the production of proactive scripts for female sexuality and erotic agency. My approach draws energy from a third-wave feminist line of attack that seeks new and intriguing ways to deconstruct residual narratives of patriarchy and to produce and reproduce new sexual scripts from an erotically empowering and sexually proactive standpoint.

Chapter One

Flipping the Sexual Script:
The Social Construction of Sexuality

Now I'ma flip some script to you so you could give love to me.
Sex is the ultimate conjugation of the verb "TO BE"

—Jessica Holter

In the third episode of the hit television show *House*, Dr. Allison Cameron discusses the physiological dynamism and implicit danger that accompany sex:

Sex could kill you. Do you know what the human body goes through when you have sex? Pupils dilate, arteries constrict, core temperature rises, heart races, blood pressure skyrockets, respiration becomes rapid and shallow, the brain fires bursts of electrical impulses from nowhere to nowhere. Secretions spit out of every gland and the muscles tense and spasm like you're lifting three times your body weight. That's violent, that's ugly, and that's messy. And if God hadn't made it unbelievably fun, the human race would have died out eons ago.

Dr. Cameron's penetrating depiction of sex as a violent, explosive act explains why people commonly regard sex as primarily a physiological phenomenon. Arrays of sexual products in the marketplace including perfumes, pheromones, sexy clothes, and all sorts of aphrodisiacs promise to bring the "animal" out of potential customers, supporting the notion that sex is fiercely primal and biological. But more and more scholars are giving attention to the ways in which sex is intensely sociological.

Sociologists explore sexuality as a system of organization and social stratification, examining how the ways in which we think about, experience, and embody the erotic, sex, and sexual identities result from social processes in all areas of social life. While acknowledging that physiological proclivities and psychological components have some bearing on sexual identity and

1

performance, sociologists regard sex, sexuality, and the erotic as acutely
social phenomena. Prior to the 1970s, sociologists rarely addressed sexuality
from a theoretical perspective, leaving the topic to a variety of psychoanalysts,
biologists, and sex experts who conceived of sexuality as the expansion of biological and environmental causes (Escoffier 2004). Though Michel Foucault
([1976] 1980) often receives credit for conveying sexuality as a progression
of discursive construction, John Gagnon and William Simon's book, *Sexual
Conduct: The Social Sources of Human Sexuality*, underscores how social
processes and sexual scripts shape, interpret, and guide sex, sexuality, and the
erotic, before Foucault's contribution. Gagnon and Simon portray sexuality as
contested locations of social performances, hence discussing sexuality not as
the coalesced result of biological instincts and social repression, but as something humans socially construct. Prior to the publication of *Sexual Conduct* in
1973, no theorists of sexuality interpret sexual behavior as so entirely social
(Escoffier 2004). Sociologists since Gagnon and Simon have rejected and
continue to reject the assumption that sexuality is biologically gendered, that
men and women are sexually poles apart, and that this gender difference is
unswerving across societies (Schwartz and Rutter 1998; Epstein 2007).

Gagnon and Simon's dramaturgical metaphor, "the script," for sexual conduct has three dimensions: cultural scenarios, interpersonal scripting, and intrapsychic scripting. Cultural scenarios reflect shared guides that exist at the
societal level as collective narratives for sex roles and acceptable practice. Interpersonal scripting involves a process that transforms the sexual participant
from functioning solely as an actor to operating as an ongoing scriptwriter,
maneuvering the materials of applicable cultural scenarios into scripts for
performance in specific situations (Simon and Gagnon 1984). Intrapsychic
scripting involves the most mysterious and contingent aspects of our sexual
selves wherein individual desires emerge and relate to social meanings and
expectations. Gagnon and Simon present individual social actors as "lay sociologists" who "possess and exploit culturally received sets of explanations
for their own and others' behavior" (Gagnon 2004: 62), drawing from past
experiences as resources to engage present performances. Their three dimensions of scripting theory challenge sociological approaches that make social
structure the focal point of the production of human behavior, recognizing the
contingency of sexual fetishes, desires, and expectations, thus demonstrating
that sexuality is a dynamic process involving social actors negotiating cultural scenarios with varying interpretations and performances.

The fact that Gagnon and Simon's scripting theory introduces social constructionist logic to the study of human sexuality does not imply a connection
to the German constructionist tradition of Alfred Schutz, Peter Berger, or
Thomas Luckmann. Gagnon and Simon's schema aligns more closely with

the pragmatists and symbolic interactionist traditions. But their scripting theory offers a social constructionist approach to sexuality, among various reasons, because it: 1) locates the significance of sex in the construction of identity and the implication of socio-cultural factors in the experience of sex; 2) deconstructs the conception of a precise binary between "natural" and "unnatural" expressions of sexuality; 3) challenges the classical sociological assumption that society constitutes a natural or objective reality that frames all aspects of social life; and 4) disputes the representation of sexuality as a treacherous influence that society must suppress to safeguard the social order (Epstein 2007), emphasizing that social actors implicate themselves in producing sexuality like any other facet of human interaction and self-identity. With the third point, in particular, Gagnon and Simon converge with the German constructionist tradition, and the fourth point shows how scripting theory recalibrates what Gayle Rubin (1992) calls the "misplaced scale" in which society imputes upon sexuality an exceptional quality or emphasis, by treating sex as just another construction of human identity and experience.

Gagnon and Simon's scripting theory quickly emerges as the preeminent model of social scientific inquests into human sexuality. Sociologists of sexuality add intriguing variations by analyzing the multifaceted historical crossing points between sexual theory and sexual politics (Weeks 1985), transformations in how people form intimate unions (Laumann et al. 2007), the macro politics of sexual knowledge-making (Epstein 2007), the ways in which people construct themselves as sexual beings vis-à-vis the manner in which sexual selves are socially constructed (Plante 2007), and how technological innovations like the proliferation and marketing of sex drugs influence scripts for sexual experience and pleasure (Tiefer 2007).

Like all social constructionists, scripting theorists maintain that social meanings shape and help interpret all physical activities regarding sex and the erotic, contending that not much regarding human behavior is wholly spontaneous. In this way, mental rehearsals of sexualized situations, masturbation fantasies, memories, sexual desires, expectations, etc. produce and depend on scripts that frame improvised sexual performances, tastes, and stimulus from erotic experiences. Potential sex partners depend on scripts to meet and negotiate erotic interactions, and utilize those scripts to judge sexual performances. A person cannot assess how well his or her partner performs sexually without the influence of scripts to set expectations and grade their execution. This does not deny that biological realities influence erotic activity, but rather emphasizes how scripts interpret, shape, and respond to inward drives and biological proclivities. Scripting theorists recognize that even seemingly natural acts like falling in love or enjoying an orgasm depend on sexual scripts to derive meaning and shape the experience as love or as orgasm. One could go so far as to contend that without scripts on sexual consent, acts such as rape and pedophilia become mere sexual behavior. As Simon and Gagnon put it, the script is the mise-en-scène of desire, transforming sheer sexual behavior into meaningful sexual conduct (1984).

Catherine MacKinnon's (1989) classic contribution to feminist theory reveals the ways that what we know (epistemology) shapes and is shaped by social power in terms of gender stratification. In contrast to scripting theorists who see sexual definitions as always subject to local interpretations, MacKinnon takes a more structural approach, depicting sexuality as a discursive system that occupies an all-encompassing and decisive social space for men's supremacy and governance and women's subordination, implying that all knowledge about sex, sexuality, and the erotic is inextricably linked with men's domination over women. MacKinnon's analytic framework treats female sexuality and women's erotic experience like objects floating in a vast sea of male domination, leaving no room for individual agency. Women, according to MacKinnon's formulation, cannot avoid participating in male domination by engaging in erotic activity.

While MacKinnon offers valuable contributions toward understanding how discourses on sex and sexuality produce and reflect structural arrangements and sexual stratification, her formulation lacks a mechanism by which societies can change or improvise from traditional assumptions of gender or sexual stratification. In other words, she cannot account for the fact that new sexual narratives often replace traditional ones. For example, MacKinnon explains the 1960s revolution of gender and sexual roles as a ploy to perpetuate male domination through sex rather than as women rejecting bourgeois or Victorian constraints on female sexuality in exchange for new interpretations of gendered sexual scripts and performances. MacKinnon closes the door to women acting on behalf of their own erotic interests.

In contrast, social constructionists examine the manner by which individuals navigate and negotiate their sexual lives, placing far less emphasis on social structure as an all-encompassing and constraining force. While recognizing that social forces influence individual decisions, social constructionists also allow for women to make choices that subvert dominant rules and expectations, giving space for transformations such as those that took place in the 1960s and beyond. Structural forces and institutional arrangements influence but do not necessarily enslave social actors, who often appropriate prevailing scripts differently and construct discursive strategies to supplant dominant approaches to the topics of sexuality, sex, and the erotic. Like most social constructionist approaches, scripting theory allows for agency and change, giving attention to the ways new cultural scenarios on marriage, love, fidelity, sexual experimentation, etc. replace traditional ones.

Scripting theory can contribute to feminism by emphasizing that "sex roles and rules vary according to gender norms and the sexual social process" (James 2006: 49), or more importantly, that the "sexual self" develops because of the preceding formation of a gendered self (Jackson 2007). Scripting theory offers feminists a more hopeful framework, suggesting that women can achieve greater liberation in society through discursive revolutions. Hence, for its ability to account for variability and social change, scripting theory remains forceful and secure as a descriptive schema for sexual conduct that is responsive to globally changing historical and cultural surroundings (Simon and Gagnon 2003), and as a useful heuristic to challenge regimes of male domination.

The United States is a society with elevated levels of sexual variability at both individual and cultural levels (Gagnon 2004), and scripting theory helps sociologists to consider the ways local performances of sexuality vary in different social contexts. By viewing sexuality from the eyehole of scripting theory, sociologists steer clear of the essentialist assumption that there is a "true" or "correct" male or female sexuality, and instead portray sex, sexuality, and the erotic as cultural products mediated and processed through social relations and interactions with institutions like the media, religion, education, etc. Sociologists locate how scripts for sexuality and the erotic socialize people to accept particular behaviors and perspectives as "normal" and "proper" (Tiefer 1995).

Erotic Revolutionaries argues that scripting theory can be useful to feminists in creating awareness of ways in which sexual narratives influence women's behavior to reinforce or subvert male domination. The fact that sex, sexuality, and the erotic are social constructions means that we view the manifestation of definitions of sexual normality and deviance within the context of the emergent discursive performances of social life (Simon 1996). This implies that some people will have more power than others in formulating and perpetuating these compositions. Scripting theory constantly reminds us not to take our (and other people's) constructions of sexuality too seriously and to consider always the potential for vested interests lurking behind sexual scripts.

Proponents of scripting theory acknowledge that sexuality and discourse are irrevocably linked, considering the strategic ways certain constructions support and reproduce particular political interests. Put simply, scripting theorists observe sexuality from the vantage point that "sexual acts have no meaning in and of themselves" (Fischer 2006: 51). Hence, one might suggest that my depiction of sexuality as mediated through scripts and performances leaves me with no grounds as a feminist to reject one approach to sexuality over another since both would qualify as discursive (and hence subjective)

accomplishments. Such estimation would judge my alliance between feminism and scripting theory as disloyal to my supposition that all definitions
of sexuality, sex, and the erotic are contingent and socially constructed. In
response, I do concede that scripting theory is my sociological technique for
constructing the world rather than empirically discovering it, and that by providing a counter-narrative against patriarchal limitations on female sexuality,
I am no less guilty of deploying a discursive strategy than my opponents. In
other words, I recognize that my prescriptive vision of female sexual exploration and autonomy cannot pretend a closer proximity to the true essence of
female sexuality, but rather what I judge to be a more viable construction of
sexuality for women. So my feminist perspective cannot reflect durable realities about sexuality and women, even while I advocate strategies to subvert
traditional discourses that I deem less beneficial to women.

So then, my feminist schema in relation to black female liberation from
the tyranny of bourgeois middle-class scripts is my own discursive creation,
reflecting no objective reality about the "true" nature of sexuality or black
womanhood (as if such a true nature exists). Yet acknowledging that all forms
of sexuality are social constructions does not preclude me from presenting
particular prescriptions for black sexual politics as intriguing alternatives for
women constrained by a sterile conformity to the politics of respectability.
Moreover, I can prefer one script to another without having to sustain my
preference with an objective template for sexuality. Thus, endorsing third-
wave feminist scripts as superior to others does not repudiate my constructionist conviction concerning the social location of all sexual scripts.

Promoting a distinct mode of sexual politics while maintaining a constructionist approach is no different from filmmaker and self-proclaimed New
York City sycophant Woody Allen advising a tourist to spend all of her time
in Manhattan to enjoy the fullest sense of the New York experience. Upon
hearing such advice, a native of Park Slope might try to interject that Brook-
lyn, not Manhattan, is the quintessence of New York City. Another casual
observer might try to convince this tourist that Staten Island is the best New
York has to offer. If intellectually honest, Woody Allen and his two detractors will admit that there is no objective barometer for deciphering which
borough captures the "true" essence of New York. But such an admission
would not preclude them from continuing to employ all of their subjective
powers to persuade the tourist their particular borough best embodies the *sine
qua non* of New York.

Similarly, just because I perceive sexuality as a social construction does
not imply that I suppose that all constructions are uniformly beneficial, in the
same way that as a native New Yorker myself, I do not regard all boroughs
equal. Just as I would advise someone to spend more time in Manhattan than

Staten Island, I would encourage a woman to reject sexual scripts that give her less options than men in exploring erotic adventures. A constructionist standpoint avoids essentialist language but still acknowledges that pragmatic realities are at play with every decision. Hence, just as I would further query the New York tourist, "Why limit yourself to Staten Island when you can visit all five boroughs?" I too petition women: "Why let gendered double standards dictate your erotic sensibilities when you can enjoy a fuller range of sexual possibilities?"

My strong polemical stance against sexual assault demonstrates this point more clearly. While I unequivocally find rape appalling, my social constructionist framework leads me to consider sexual assault as having no intrinsic moral content. In other words, I acknowledge that my own particular paradigm frames my revulsion against non-consensual sexual activity. From such a constructionist perspective, I would have to acknowledge that an antebellum slave owner, for example, has just as much discursive grounds to conceptualize sexual assault as an acceptable social practice, as I have to impute rape with deviance and terror, because sexual deviance has no reality *sui generis*, but rather is evaluated and defined through discursive strategies. But while I accept that all moral discourses about rape involve sexual scripts and that all sexual scripts are inherently subjective, I am no less compelled to persuade people to embrace a particular narrative that frames rape as a repugnant act, without being inconsistent to my constructionist position. Similarly, while I accept black female sexuality as a narrative construction, I am no less constrained to persuade black women (or all women for that matter) to reject discursive strategies that restrict their sexual toolkits on gendered grounds; I am not claiming that such an achievement brings them closer to a true essence of female sexuality, but rather that agency and autonomy trump a politics of respectability rooted in gendered double standards.

This book represents an unprecedented nexus between feminist sexual politics and social constructionist theorizing. I demonstrate that scripting theory is a useful analytic to challenge feminists not to economize around accepted wisdom of a politically correct sanitized female sexuality, but rather to be adamant that women are sexual subjects, actors, and agents. Since much of our social acceptability is contingent upon how well we perform our designed gender roles, how we define those roles has imminent social consequence. To rearticulate, since power operates in part through social norms, and gender norms influence how women set their own potentialities and gauge those around them, feminist activity should focus great attention toward deconstructing oppressive gender norms as a form of political action (McLaren 2002).

A productive locale for future sexual scripts research is the function that the media plays in composing or confronting beliefs in the cultural, interpersonal, and intrapsychic realms (Dworkin and O' Sullivan 2007). This work looks to women in popular culture as purveyors of subversive sexual scripts that undermine traditional scripts that delimit female sexual agency and empowerment. Rather than portraying sexy black divas of popular culture as victims or mere objects of the male gaze, I depict them as feminists who create new scripts and carve out new space for female sexual subjectivity by exerting distinctive brands of sexual empowerment. I analyze subjects who negotiate their identities and careers in a world in which, on the one hand, the residual effects of male domination place borders on the space they have for individuality and creativity, but conversely in which they wield far more power to transgress those borders and create new space with sexual discourse, sensuality, and erotic artistry than black women of any previous generation.

Whereas some critics view popular culture as a culture industry irrevocably committed to reproducing discourses of male sexual domination, I join a growing cohort of scholars approaching media to explore the important connection between sexuality and feminist empowerment. My central contention is that popular culture can function as a location for feminist politics by affording women access to subversive sexual scripts and new discourses of sexuality to renegotiate their sexual histories. As popular culture makes multiple discourses available to people, feminist scholars can sift through these representations and distinguish between those they deem subversive to patriarchy and those representations they regard as ultimately empowering. For example, when a movie like *She's Gotta Have It* emerges in the 1980s with a character like Nola Darling who undermines traditional sexual narratives, women can refer to Nola's seditious acts when constructing, interpreting, and reconsidering their own sexual experiences and desires. Similarly when Lynn Searcy, a smart, funny, and talented character on the television show *Girlfriends* flaunts her sexual power, objectifies male acquaintances, brags about masturbating in the shower, dates or kisses a woman, and finds almost every imaginable way to defy the politics of respectability, she offers her audience new ways to imagine and negotiate black female sexuality and new tools to employ in their sexual repertoires.

Whereas less progressive sexual scripts often put the onus on women to coddle men's erotic imaginations, erotic revolutionaries like Zane, Hilda Hutcherson, Alexyss Tylor, and Janet Jackson teach women that it is okay to flip the sexual script, so to speak, and evaluate men rather than hyper-analyzing their own sexual performances. Tyra Banks, LaDawn Black, Sommore, and Mo'Nique reject traditional sexual scripts that make men the locus of concern for women, and deploy subversive scripts that encourage women to make sexual demands on men, be proactive in sustaining their relationship to sexual pleasure, and negotiate sexual interactions on their own terms. These erotic revolutionaries teach black women that a politics of respectability is no longer an acceptable touchstone.

Hence this work forges an important connection between subversive discourse, media representation, and feminist sexual politics. This jives well with these unremitting feminist mandates: to stir up "gender trouble" with discursive acts against society's prescribed rules and expectations for how men and women are supposed to act (Butler 1990); to take up the task of "gender maneuvering" by violating popular presumptions about gender and sexuality that limit the potentialities of women (Schippers 2002); and to "bring wreck" against patriarchy with rhetorical acts of resistance (Pough 2004). Erotic revolutionaries stir up gender trouble, generate gender maneuvering, and bring wreck into the public square by providing a variety of images and narratives as themes accessible to confronting, redrafting, and recoding gender expectations on sexuality.

Chapter Two

Sultry Divas of Pop and Soul:
Janet, Beyoncé, and Jill

I was told they would be happy to go ahead with it if I were to take the sensual songs off the album. And I thought, "Wow, that's weird." Here I am talking about love and expressing myself in a way I feel at least most of us do in the bedroom, and it is something so beautiful, so positive and wonderful, yet they want me to put a blindfold over the public's eyes about this.

—Janet Jackson

One day I'll be older and not quite as cute, with tits not as perky and an ass not as round. But right now? I'll be damned if I'm going to hide what God gave me.

—Kelis

Few people in contemporary American society can doubt music's powerful impact on our daily experience. Advertisers use infectious songs to sell products, athletes listen to soundtracks with kinetic beats to pump themselves up before games, movie directors enrich love scenes with melodic scores, lovers use music to create the right ambiance, and educators utilize music as a method to teach youngsters everything from math to science. In *The Rest is Noise: Listening to the Twentieth Century*, Alex Ross demonstrates how music reflects and shapes the cataclysmic events of the twentieth century. Whether it is Negro spirituals during slavery, protest songs during the civil rights movement, or catchy tunes from the Spice Girls during the 1990s girl power movement, music is often on the cusp of political and social change. It should not surprise us then that music has a profound impact on black sexual politics.

African-American singers and musicians challenged the sexual politics of their day in various ways. Layli Phillips and Marla Stewart contend that "blues music has stood as the accepted historical repository for discourse of sexual diversity within the black community" (2009: 23). Similarly, Angela Davis analyzes the careers of several African-American women blues singers of the early twentieth century, arguing that the representations of love and sexuality in women's blues often subvert mainstream scripts regarding women and being in love. Davis shows how blues legends like Gertrude "Ma" Rainey and Bessie Smith outshine men with their amazing sexual voracity and write songs that allude to female sexual independence and assertiveness:

> These blues women had no qualms about announcing female desire. Their songs express women's intention to "get their loving." Such affirmations of sexual autonomy and open expressions of female desire give historical voice to possibilities of equality not articulated elsewhere. Women's blues and the cultural politics lived out in the careers of the blues queens put these new possibilities on the historical agenda. (1998: 24)

Davis presents female blues singers as proto-feminists and independent women who exhibit collective modes of black consciousness, demand sexual agency, and assert sexual equality with men.

Similarly, Hazel Carby (1999) contends that the blues genre empowered women singers with safe space to maneuver through patriarchal terrain as sexual subjects and to address the contradictions of feminism, sexuality, and power. Carby reveals how the blues offer black women an alternative form of representation that fights the patriarchal objectification of female sexuality, but does so while reclaiming black women and their bodies as powerful sexual subjects. This transitory space for the free expression and control of black female sexuality through blues songs dissolves when the "race records" industry that records them fizzles out during the Depression, and blues women like Ethel Waters and Hattie McDaniels leave the music industry to transcend the Hollywood films "where they occupied not a privileged but a subordinate space and articulated not the possibilities of black female sexual power but the 'Yes, Ma'am' of the black maid" (Carby 1999: 11). This safe space for provocative sexual politics through music reemerges in the 1950s and continues to pervade the music industry today to the extent that subsequent singers who manipulate their representation as sexual subjects are invariably indebted to blues singers of the past.

Few women in the 1920s and '30s push the limits of black female sexuality like sultry singer and dancer Josephine Baker. Realizing her seductive performances are too risqué for American sensibilities, she leaves her homeland to become a world-famous entertainer in France. Alluding to her sensual power and erotic performances, Brenda Dixon Gottschild compares Baker to contemporary pop vocal icon Madonna:

Like Madonna, she personified the agency, power, and autonomy of the female performing body both onstage and off. At times she was a free agent, setting the rules (or disrupting established ones) for a liberated, self-driven sexuality. Like Madonna, she didn't break the stereotype but "worked it" and challenged it from within rather than protesting it from an oppositional feminist perspective. (2003: 155)

Unlike Americans during the swing era, the French had the savoir-faire to distinguish something refreshingly modern and special about Josephine Baker's seductive performances and free sexuality. Baker is not simply the object of the male gaze, but the powerful subject of a fresh new brand of eroticism.

As part of the sexual revolution of the 1960s, black girl groups like the Shirelles and the Supremes touch upon female longing and sexual desire, encouraging girls and women to be proactive in their love lives. In *Where the Girls Are: Growing Up Female with the Mass Media*, Susan Douglas (1995) explains how girl groups of the 1960s offer women different personas to challenge a male-dominated society. Douglas believes that white women like herself owe cultural arrears to black girl groups for smuggling a taste of sexual liberation into middle class America and for generating a more sexually curious teen girl culture. On similar lines, philosopher Cornel West argues:

Listening to Motown records in the 1960s or dancing to hip-hop music in the 1990s may not lead one to question the sexual myths of black women and men, but when white and black kids buy the same billboard hits and laud the same athletic heroes, the result is often a shared cultural space where some humane interaction takes place. (1999: 515)

Douglas and West confirm bell hooks' (1992) contention that popular music is a valuable cultural setting for discussing black sexuality. But whereas hooks delves into popular culture to identify oppressive representations of black female sexuality, Douglas and I focus our attention on the ways in which popular culture can function as a location of feminist politics by affording women access to subversive sexual scripts and new discourses of sexuality to renegotiate their sexual identities.

Since the sexual revolution of the 1960s, Diana Ross, Aretha Franklin, Anita Baker, and Tina Turner delve into themes that link romance and sexual pleasure, while contemporary black female vocalists explore new erotic frontiers. Few black singers awakened the sexual imagination of our nation more than Janet Jackson. It's difficult to imagine how the precocious young girl who plays Penny on the television comedy *Good Times* in the 1970s evolves into the sultry pop-diva of the 1990s and beyond.

After her first two CDs generate moderate buzz from music critics, Janet joins forces with music producers Jimmy Jam and Terry Lewis in 1986 to release her breakthrough CD entitled *Control*. *Control* sparks the beginning of Janet's girl-power sensuality with edgy songs. In "Nasty," she demands her love interest to be a gentleman and show her respect, and in her title song "Control," she tells us she doesn't want to rule the world, she just wants to rule her life. In "Let's Wait Awhile," she says let's take it slow and get to know each other, and she promises to be worth the wait. While her next album *Rhythm Nation* adds to her preeminence with socially conscious messages about poverty and racial harmony, her subsequent CDs do much to brand her as one of the most sexually stimulating vocalists of the 1990s.

In 1993, Janet Jackson poses topless on the cover of the September issue of *Rolling Stone* with another person's hands covering her breasts. This cover shot is reminiscent of an earlier photo that year for her self-entitled CD *Janet*. The tantalizing image foreshadows the erotic lyrics that appear in singles throughout the CD. In "That's the Way Love Goes" she promises to take her man to places he's never been. She urges him to reach out and feel her body; slow down because he's got her there all night; to go deeper, and that he feels so good she's going to cry. In "Any Time Any Place" she is burning with overwhelming passion, telling her man that she doesn't care if people are standing around, she wants him now. In "You Want This" she demands for her man to work it because she's not going to accept a sub-par performance. A proactive participant, she coaches her men throughout the sexual interaction.

The eroticism intensifies with Janet Jackson's next CD *The Velvet Rope* in 1997. In her song "Go Deep" she talks about her man freaking her from behind and making him scream and moan. In the video for "I Get Lonely" Janet rips open her shirt exposing a black lace bra and continues dancing as she sings about needing to resolve her loneliness. In "My Need" she expresses an irresistible desire for a sexual fix, promising her suitor that they don't have to talk about any promises, all she wants is to make love like it is their last time. "Free Xone" encourages safe space for homosexual exploration as two guys meet on a plane and a girl meets girl, loses girl and gets the cute girl back; the song provides a rare incident in which a popular black vocalist explores romantic or sensual energy outside the contours of heteronormativity, making it a significant song in black sexual politics.

Her next album *All for You* in 2001 features a thirty-five-year-old Janet after her divorce and the lyrics of her songs reflect a newly single woman's friskiness, as does the cover shot, which displays her lying in bed with no more than a sheet shielding her nude body. In "Would You Mind" she tells her man she's going to kiss, touch, lick, taste, bathe, ride, and feel him deep inside her, and how his lips on her make her all juicy. She ends the song by requesting that he come inside of her and let his juices flow deep in her passion. In the title track "All for You" she's at a party with her girls and she rolls up on a dude and compliments him about his "package" and tells him she's going to have to ride it tonight—a bold and proactive sexual maneuver for even a twenty-first century woman. As the song proceeds she maintains control, issuing detailed instructions on just how the guy should approach her and maintain the correct disposition in her presence. While Janet generally eschews profanity, she ends the song "Love Scene (Ooh Baby)" by telling her man how she feels "when you're fucking me." In "Trust a Try" Janet is soft and understanding while consoling her man because his ex broke his heart, and yet firm and direct while warning him not to distrust her and smother her. Janet's proactive feedback to her partners about what pleases and displeases her is a recurring phenomenon in her songs. Her female personas are not passive dupes, but active participants in their relationships in everything from venting frustration to directing sexual interplay and initiating sexual encounters, thus offering women assertive sexual scripts to mediate their own sexual interplay.

Although Janet's next CD *Damita Jo* is more personal and intimate, she turns up the sexual heat even higher than her previous efforts on many of the songs. She offers little refinement in "Sexhibition" and tells her mate that she wants to "sexplore" him and take him on a sexcapade. She says she does not have to figure him out because she basically just wants to turn him out and drive his ass crazy. Here Janet shows women it is okay to treat men as sex tools for a change. "Moist" is no less restrained in that she compares her lust to a waterfall, and tells her lover that his touch makes her scream and his whispers arouse her. "Moist" reflects Janet's frequent use of liquid metaphors to illustrate her sexual arousal. In "All Nite" she's intoxicated, stimulated, and feels so X-rated, telling her man to spank that back door and drive her like a Porsche. In "Thinking Bout My Ex," while she laments breaking her new boyfriend's heart, she nevertheless informs him that when she's holding him at night, kissing him, lying with him, and touching him gently, her mind is actually on her ex. In "I Want You," her body is crying for her man to have his way with her, anytime, anywhere, anyway. The sexual allusions in her song "Warmth" alone show why she is the erotic queen of pop.

In 2004 Janet draws a groundswell of media attention not just for *Damita Jo*, but when Justin Timberlake rips off part of her costume at the end of their performance, exposing her breast to a live television audience during the *Super Bowl Half-Time Show*. Whether the infamous incident is an intentional act of defiance or an actual clothing malfunction, it exposes the gendered double standard concerning how the American public responds to male and female bodies. Janet's breast incites hundreds of thousands of calls from angry viewers and vigorous debates by conservative media watchdogs concerning the topic of indecent exposure, while there's no principled injunction against the plethora of bare-chested men who pervade our television screens in everything from dramas and sitcoms to boxing matches and World Wrestling Entertainment. This may cause the objective onlooker to question just what it is that deems Janet's breast a colossal threat to society in comparison to the utter acceptability of the male breast. The answer resides in the fact that obscenity is socially defined, and obscenity laws support patriarchal power relations within society (Godfrey 2006). Although it might be somewhat disheartening that Janet later apologizes instead of protecting her right to expose herself in the same manner that men do, her Super Bowl surprise is nevertheless a treasonable act in a society that, as Susan Bordo points out, tacitly and legally demands women to discipline their breasts (1993).

Janet refuses to turn down the sensual energy in her next CD, *20 Y.O.*, which commemorates twenty years since coming out with her first marketable effort, *Control*. In "So Excited" her body is in overdrive dying to have her man inside of her, and she promises to open up her "spot" for him as well as to keep his body thumping. In "Show Me" she rebukes her man for not listening to her because he is kissing and moving too fast, and she punishes him by making him work harder for it. In "Day Break" she's waiting for everyone in her family to fall asleep so she can sneak out and rendezvous with her lover. Many of the songs on this CD share the common theme of a woman aggressively demanding her partner to fulfill mental, emotional, and sexual needs.

In February 2008 Janet appears on CNN's show *Larry King Live* to promote her new CD *Discipline*. Discussing it with Janet, host Larry King mentions, "Some of the lyrics are pretty racy; are you attracted to that?" Janet tells King that she writes about life experiences and celebrates her womanhood and sensual side with her songs. King could be alluding to any number of tracks on *Discipline* when he suggests her lyrics are racy. In "Feedback" she puts her body on display for a peep show in which her partner is free to explore her erotic zones. In "Rock with You" she commands her partner to be silent while she "talks" to his body; and in "2Nite" she is soaking wet waiting to give her partner something he will never forget (liquidity reappears as Janet's choice metaphor for arousal). Her song "The 1" features the never-shy hip-hop starlet Missy Elliot questioning a man about his penis size, and proposing her services as another lover to get freaky undercover.

Janet Jackson goes from writing love songs about relationships and regret early in her career, to articulating the heat and intensity of female passion and sexuality in her later years. Like Madonna, Janet interacts aggressively with male dancers in videos and concerts and remains a vibrant symbol of sexual freedom. Whether it's tying down a man to a gurney to give him an erotic lap dance during a live show or posing on the cover of the October 2006 issue of FHM in white bikini bottoms and a matching white strap covering only one breast, Janet's songs and antics convey to women that there is room to be bold and sexy. Her brash sensuality and erotic lyrics disseminate discursive strategies for women to be at ease with their sexual longings and demands.

As Janet approaches the twilight of her reign as erotic queen of pop, Beyoncé Knowles emerges as her likely successor. To watch her imitate Marilyn Monroe singing "Diamonds are a Girl's Best Friend" in a television commercial for Emporia Armani, appear on the cover of the 2007 *Sports Illustrated Swimsuit Edition*, model the New Infallible Never Fail Lip Colour for L'Oreal, sport a sultry leather jumpsuit as Foxy Cleopatra in the hit movie *Austin Powers*, or grab her crotch while performing at the 2010 Grammy Awards is to see why Beyoncé is one of the most recognized sex symbols in pop culture.

We initially observe the seeds of a Janet-like allure in Beyoncé early on when she appears as the lead vocalist of the hit girl group Destiny's Child. Her mother Tina Knowles crafts an image and style for Destiny's Child reminiscent of the elegance and sophistication of the classic days of Motown: the long slinky dresses sported by the Supremes, the apple hats worn by the Jackson 5, the funky colors rocked by Sly and the Family Stone, and the fabulous outfits Cher wore on her hit show in the seventies (Knowles 2002). Beyoncé hits her stride as a teenager with signature blond hair, curvy hips and thighs, slim waist, and a growing booty. She performs on stage and appears in videos sporting exotic retrogrades like traditional Indian saris, antique chokers, and amulet necklaces, along with contemporary urban looks with fun belts, belly chains, customized t-shirts with rhinestones, and thigh-high boots. The movie *One Million Years B.C.*, which makes Raquel Welch a pinup icon, inspires the sexy fur ensemble sported by Destiny's Child in the video for "Survivor." Destiny's Child perform in bikini tops and belly-baring shirts, granting sizzle to army fatigue outfits long before camouflage comes en vogue. But it is not until Beyoncé leaves the group and embarks on her solo career that she achieves ultimate pop-diva sex appeal.

Beyoncé's upgrade to sex-symbol status erupts on the sets of her sassy video for "Crazy in Love," the hit song she records with hip-hop legend and eventual hubby, Jay Z. She stakes a claim to the sexy diva throne the moment she sashays across the street in those blue tight Daisy Duke shorts and white tank top, and shakes her rear in her now infamous "uh-oh" dance. Her performances in the video and in songs from her solo CDs signify Beyoncé's new liberated image and carve out safe space for the emergence of Sasha, her sexy alter ego. In her hit song "Naughty Girl" she confesses that a guy has got her feeling sexy and nasty, while "Get Me Bodied" empowers millions of women to hit the dance floor feeling sexy and lustful and to forget all their worries and yield to the seductive temptations of their sensuality. In "Be With You" she promises her man that tonight's the night all his fantasies will come true; and in "Suga Mama" she objectifies her man by providing him with financial sustenance in return for sensual favors. Like Janet, Beyoncé takes on varying personas: she's bursting with passion and lust; she's chastising her man for infidelity and betrayal; she's lonely; she's basking in her own seductive powers. Her catchy hooks become anthems that reflect the sentiments of many young women. She draws from an array of symbolic resources at her disposal to express herself as free, sensual, and alive.

In Los Angeles in 2007, Beyoncé records her live show "The Beyoncé Experience," which includes over thirty performance pieces. Her sexy alter ego Sasha is in rare form as she shakes, twists, and gyrates to simulate sex moves. She comes out belly dancing and wearing a bikini top and island skirt to greet Sean Paul, singing "Baby Boy," and moments later she's on stage surrounded by five chiseled men wearing army fatigues. She dances, shakes, trembles, screams, jumps, poses with her hand on hip, smiles, and captivates her audience with a visual orgy. Like Janet Jackson, she presents sensuality as power; she is in full control over the men who appear onstage as well as her own erotic energy. Her movements exude eroticism and her voice transmits vibrations of sensual momentum. Similarly, in the video for "Single Ladies," a big hit from her third solo CD, Beyoncé shows us the booty shaking, gyrations, and sexy poses that signify her as the new Janet.

But there is a more telling way to measure Beyoncé's impact on sexuality besides listening to songs from her platinum-selling CDs, watching her live performances, numerous commercials, movies, videos, or gazing at her bikini-clad body in the pages of the *Sports Illustrated Swimsuit Edition*. Just venture out to any dance club and observe the change that takes place in many of the young women as soon as the DJ plays one of Beyoncé s songs. You will probably notice that something almost paranormal takes over young women, akin to the Holy Ghost enveloping a "church mother" at a Pentecostal revival. These women almost instinctively begin to dance more freely as if taking on the song's sexual anointing. While mouthing the words and mimicking her movements, such women occupy safe space to be seductive and bask in their sensuality while following Beyoncé s lead. After the song concludes, catharsis is achieved as the sexual anointing recedes and the women revert to their previous personas.

Some critics project sexy pop divas like Beyoncé as sex objects rather than proactive subjects constructing their own sexual representation. Patricia Hill

Collins argues that black female vocalists like Beyoncé who appear in leop-ard-skin bikinis and bare midriffs are products of a Western culture that ex-ploits a stereotype of African American women as oversexed beings (2004). Similarly, pop vocalist Kelis discusses how the music industry pressures women to exploit their sensuality, often using their talent as their secondary feature. "Sex sells. It's sad but true," she explains (Kelis 2005: 103). But Kelis flips the sexual script by proudly defending her decision to use her sex appeal to enhance her music career and express herself as a woman:

> America is all about what is appealing to the eye. And I have a better chance of getting where I want looking the way I do than trying to be a burlap-wearing, waving-incense-wherever-I-go woman. God bless those who go that route, but it's not for me. (Ibid)

It appears that Kelis' views on female objectification are refreshingly nu-anced as she admits to experiencing some personal angst on the one hand, yet seemingly adheres to Elizabeth Wurtzel's rousing assertion that "putting out one's pretty power, one's pussy power, one's sexual energy out there for pop-ular consumption no longer makes you a bimbo—it makes you smart" (1998: 11). In a music industry where women generally lack agency in videos for male hip-hop artists, rockers, and R&B singers, it is noteworthy that women like Beyoncé and Kelis control much of their own sexual self-presentation. Many feminists overlook Joanna Frueh's contention that a woman who opts to expose her body as an erogenous zone may be claiming her sexuality in ways that confront and counter sexist images of women (1996).

While Janet, Beyoncé, Kelis, and other pop stars like Ashanti, Mya and Amerie expose their flesh and relish their sexual power, Erykah Badu, India. Arie, Macy Gray, and Angie Stone represent a neo-soul movement of black female vocalists who essentially conceal their bodies while electing to place their minds and souls front and center. Neo-soul singers helped fashion a new culture of black conscious women. In almost every city nationwide you can find enclaves of head-wrap-wearing, incense-waving women who subscribe to the political, artistic, and aesthetic flavors of this burgeoning neo-soul movement. You can find them at coffee shops, spoken word venues, and lounges espousing eclectic spirituality, social consciousness, poignant critiques on life, and philosophies on love and self-respect. Neo-soul women endorse a more conservative brand of empowered sensuality that does not lend itself to erotic displays of the flesh, and hence is more suitable to black middle-class bourgeois notions of female respectability. Notwithstanding neo-soul women's refreshing spirituality and trenchant social conscious-ness, too many people make female empowerment a zero-sum game rather than celebrating the choice women have to either cover up, like Me' Shell

Ndegeocello and India.Arie, or let it all hang out, like Janet and Beyoncé; to offer messages of social consciousness like Lauryn Hill, or celebrate the power and awe of masturbation like Charlene "Tweet" Keys. As Erykah Badu demonstrates with modesty throughout her longstanding career, and nakedness in her recent controversial video "Window Seat," both covering up and exposing the goods can empower women to varying degrees and reflect sexual agency and proactive representation.

When Jill Scott bursts onto the music scene and releases her first CD, *Who Is Jill Scott? Words and Sounds, vol. 1,* music critics quickly brand the vocalist alongside the burgeoning neo-soul movement, for plausible reasons. For many, it seems natural to position Jill Scott as the anti-Janet because of the explicit contrasts between the two vocalists. While Janet is a lean, fit sex symbol displaying nimble choreography and six-pack abs, Jill is a "Philly-thick" woman who creates new spaces to project "big girls" as attractive (Neal 2003). Our thin-is-in media culture inadvertently induces many people to focus more praise and attention on the content of Jill Scott's lyrics while de-emphasizing the contours of a plus-size body that bares no skin and shows no agile dance moves like Janet. Moreover, many critics inaccurately brand Janet as a processed package, while Jill is deemed organic with her hair natural and neo-soul fashion apparel. At first glance, Jill's socially conscious lyrics and intellectualism also eclipse what many carelessly construe as Janet's erotic simplicity. It is easy, then, for music critics to trap Jill Scott inside a neo-soul box that emphasizes spirituality, self-actualization, and romantic purity. The obvious benefit of such an imprint ensures that Jill has fewer obstacles gaining acceptance as a serious songwriter and intellectual force.

So from the moment Jill Scott releases her first CD in 2000, critics hail her as a neo-soul woman of substance, and do not even entertain the possibility of dismissing her as a sex symbol. But those who place her in such a neat spiritual box often overlook the seething sexiness she flaunts in her music, poetry, personas, and even with her body. Yes Jill is positive and conscious, but she's also profoundly human and taps into an assemblage of emotions and conditions including anger, regret, fear, loneliness, and an overwhelming longing for male sexual energy. The neo-soul box often limits critics from perceiving her as the highly sensual woman she is. Truth be told, Janet Jackson is far more intellectual and socially conscious than critics and academics recognize, just as Jill unexpectedly is one of the most sensual artists around. A glance at Jill's picture in the September 2007 issue of *Essence*, where she's lying across a couch in a sizzling red velvet dress, shows her sex appeal speaking a thousand words. Like Janet, she offers contemporary women safe space for addressing and exploring a full range of female sexual desire.

Many of the songs on her first two CDs express a healthy appreciation for sex. In "Exclusively" she brags about her man breaking her off with some good extra loving in which he is licking and sucking on everything. The song depicts them lying in bed sweaty and "sex-funky" after their morning exchange of fluids has worked up a huge appetite. Ironically, when she ventures to the store to purchase breakfast, she discovers that her man does not love her exclusively, as the grocery store clerk is able to decipher his scent on her.

In "He Loves Me" she admits that when her partner touches her she loses control and that he ignites and incites her to chorus. In "It's Love" she's going crazy over the way she's sweating his loving. In "Love Rain" she divulges that being in love made "the coochie easy" and obstructs her ability to see that the relationship is taking a tragic turn. In "I'm Not Afraid" she boasts that she is not scared of being his whore. Female lust is at play in "Bedda at Home" when she claims her man is the kind of guy who breaks it down in the bedroom and curls her toes. In "Whatever" she brags that her beau puts it down in bed so powerfully that he has her climbing up a wall.

Jill's third CD *The Real Thing* is even more sexual than her first two efforts. The first song "Let It Be" is her new mandate not to let people put her music in a box (presumably she's referring to the neo-soul box), and foreshadows a new freedom and explosive sensuality throughout the CD. For example, "Epiphany" documents an entire sexual experience that begins with lusty, sweaty foreplay and ends with energetic intercourse. As her stomach meets the sheets, he plows inside her as if he's making beats, and he rides "Mount Saint Scott" until creamy lava lands on her skin and neck. She returns the favor by moving her back and hips to work him so hard that she puts him to sleep, "curled all up, spasm all in his feet." But "Epiphany" takes an existential twist as the song's anticlimax has her wondering why she feels so empty? Thus, within the nexus of a single song, Jill exposes the power of sex to produce feelings of both ultimate delight and utter desolation. Such pangs of duality are compatible with her overall impression of the ambivalence of human sexuality above and beyond surface classification. Hence Jill confirms Carole Vance's assessment that "the hallmark of sexuality is its complexity: its multiple meanings, sensations, and connections" (1992: 5).

Other songs on *The Real Thing* demonstrate an intense sensuality. She insinuates vigorous sex positions in "Crown Royal" as she arches her back, squirts "mad oil," dips her hips, and raves about both his tongue tricks and his nature being so thick. The name "Crown Royal" is an urban moniker that represents a sexually dexterous man, thus many of her fans know exactly where Jill is going with the song's recurring metaphor. In "Celibacy Blues" she compares herself to an addict needing a sexual fix and alludes to sleepless nights and wearing out the batteries of her vibrator in her desperate struggle to remain celibate. In "All I" she obsesses with the idea of sleeping with a guy, and even offers her services to be his nasty baby if he should desire.

The Moments, the Minutes, the Hours: The Poetry of Jill Scott exudes the same sexual verisimilitude embedded in many of her songs. In her poem "Independent Woman" a female protagonist masturbates while she's watching porn, constantly rewinding her favorite scene; she's independent, has no man hassles, no stress; tastes herself and pleases herself and savors the fact that her fingers don't require store-bought protection, affection, or direction. With the uneasiness in black communities with forthright discussions about masturbation (Neal 2003), Jill does much to present it as an essential device in the female sexual toolkit.

Bodies bang and grind in her poem "The Last Time," and in "Across Your Bread," the narrator's man has her thighs swelling and knees begging to part. The female protagonist of "The Downfall of a North Philly Freak" succumbs to her sexual desire for a brown tall regal sexy brotha who is "smelling good like hot sex on Sunday." "Young Buck Lovin' on the Kitchen Floor" is about spontaneous sex in the kitchen but ends with a tragic twist: the brotha who took the protagonist to heaven's gate made it sting when she peed, thus implying that he gave her more than just a good time. In "Radio Blues" the narrator asks someone to screw her, tease her, please her, and freak her; and in the poem "Old School Lovin" she tells her man to close both eyes and open his mouth and taste her original-brand sweet potato pie, if you know what she means!

No doubt, many of Jill's poems and songs envelop themes outside of sex and eroticism. Her strong message of self-reliance in songs like "One is the Magic #" and "Hate on Me," encouragement in songs like "Brotha," and poetic exhortations like "Revolutionary Man" and "Tree Like She" all raise social consciousness, inspire, and enlighten her listeners. But we must not deny that along with offering conscious messages, Jill provokes women (and men) to explore their sexual longings and desires without the shame and humiliation that is par for the course with the politics of respectability. Women in her poems and songs find themselves lusting after men, falling into temptation, and celebrating male sexual energy.

Janet, Beyoncé, and Jill construct female personas alongside a series of polarities: lustful and contemplative, aggressive and passive, seductive and seduced, predator and victim, sexually satisfied and neglected, powerful and weak. They present themselves as sensual subjects who moan and groan and ooooh and ahhh about sex and physical pleasure and also as sexual objects who men sometimes exploit. While they consistently present sexuality as an explosive force that brings much comfort, excitement, and exuberance, they

also present sexuality as a destructive power with the capacity to ruin relationships, keep women up all night, and incite people toward bitter, jealous,
and abusive states of being.

Susan Douglas reveals that the genius of pop music resides in its ability to
persuade people that they can transcend the shackles of conventional life:

> The most important thing about this music, the reason it spoke to us so power-
> fully, was that it gave voice to all the warring selves inside us struggling blindly
> and with crushing sense of insecurity, to forge something resembling a coherent
> identity (1995: 87).

Like the girl groups of the 1960s to which Douglas alludes, Janet, Beyoncé,
and Jill provide multiple templates for women to respond to the vagaries of
life, love, and libido. Sometimes their female personas are self-important and
unruly, yet other times self-abnegating and yielding. These erotic revolutionaries delight in their own sexual power while reminding women that a healthy
dose of lust can invigorate their lives.

Whether it is Tina Turner in the 1960s or Janet, Beyoncé and Jill today,
black female pop artists construct sexual scripts encouraging women to function as active agents of their own love, to demand sexual pleasure, and to
serve men notice that poor, uninspired sexual performances are not acceptable. But these vocalists also portray women in more vulnerable moments
second-guessing their own motives and intentions while expressing angst
about particular sexual experiences. Hence, black female artists present
women as complex subjects. While a feminist moralism leads many women
to conform to middle-class codes of decorum, these artists inspire women to
embrace more proactive scripts for female sexuality, ultimately illustrating
for women that sexuality and power can go hand in hand. By presenting an
extensive range of sexualized human scenarios and by furnishing everyday
life with some of its vigor, popular music organizes sexual narratives that
shape how people imagine themselves as sexual beings. Janet, Beyoncé, and
Jill provide women with copious assets for creating a sexual self, demonstrating how popular music provides notable artistic provinces to see scripting
theory at play.

Chapter Three

Confessions of a Video Vixen

I have single-handedly reshaped my culture.

—Karrine Steffans

Like it or not, we now live in a media age where talk shows, reality programs, chat rooms, and Internet blogs transform us into voyeurs of other people's sex lives. Hollywood celebrities, athletes, politicians, and business executives reveal intimate details in "tell-all" books, tabloid magazines, and television interviews. Discussing frailties and struggles with a confidant is one thing, but declaring intimate details about one's sexuality to the public is a bolder endeavor. A growing number of black women are writing essays and books that explore their sexual histories and perspectives as a means of challenging the politics of respectability.

Journalist and life coach Tara Roberts is a leading pioneer in collecting the sexual testimonies of black women as well as exposing intimate details of her own history. Believing that sexual silence threatens the very fabric of young women's lives, she is editor of *Am I the Last Virgin?: Ten African American Reflections on Sex and Love*. Among the many authors in the anthology, Roberts discusses the challenges of dealing with sexual urges and maintaining healthy relationships to preserve her virginity; Lisa Chestnut-Chapman recalls her love affair with a popular musician; Kim-Monique Johnson reveals the process of discovering lesbian feelings; and Chemin Abner-Ware recollects the tragedy of being diagnosed HIV positive and living with AIDS.

A decade later, Roberts assembles a second anthology, *What Your Mama Never Told You: True Stories About Sex and Love*, which, like her first book, engages a wide range of experiences and sexual challenges faced by young

African-American women. Roberts discusses her purpose for the book in the introduction:

> No longer is it okay for brown girls to die slow, quiet, invisible deaths around their sexuality. Since our sexuality is intricately tied in with our souls, we want to raise it up, to fortify its essential, wild, panther-like essence before it begins to shrivel and wrinkle and fold in on itself. We exorcise shame and guilt from our vocabularies and reclaim the pieces of our sexuality that have been locked away. And we declare in big, roaring voices that you have a right to know your body intimately, fully, and unapologetically, and that you should be encouraged to savor every crevice, every delicate fold, every delicious smell. (2007: xii)

The essays in this volume include discussions about first sexual experiences, a woman's relationship with her vagina, and several stories about women overcoming feelings of shame and rediscovering sexual pleasure. Roberts' anthologies provide an intriguing source of female empowerment by expanding the sexual discourse of young African-American women.

Tricia Rose wrote *Longing to Tell: Black Women Talk about Sexuality and Intimacy* in order to resolve how race, class, and gender inequality affect the way black women talk about their sexual lives. She interviews black women and interprets their views on intimacy, sex and sexuality, masturbation, orgasms, virginity, motherhood, and sexual abuse, and discovers a striking nexus between sexual experience and various facets of life and society. She writes:

> Their parents' marital relationships, their own career goals, their religious training, medical racism, poverty compounded by racism and sexism, images of black women in society, sometimes their own drug problems, all are part of the sexual story being told, not diversion from it. These sexual stories, when allowed to unfold in the context of women's lives, call out to us to see that black women share important contemporary social, political, and cultural histories with one another and share other histories with women from diverse backgrounds. (2003: 8)

Her discussants include women like Rhonda, a lesbian who conquers drug addiction and now educates other women as a social activist; Linda Rae, a middle-aged woman battling AIDS; and Luciana, who after years of engaging in unfulfilling sex, is now ready to explore her sexual desires but cannot find a partner. Their stories provide a valuable contribution to the underdeveloped narrative of black women's sexuality in America.

"In sharing our stories we have discovered that we are women who enjoy being sexual," claims psychotherapist Julia Boyd in her book *Embracing the Fire: Sisters Talk about Sex* (1997: 4). Her book is the result of her own endeavor to recognize how the messages about sex and relationships spread by older women are incompatible with her own life experiences. Boyd weaves the testimonies and perspectives of several of her friends alongside her own personal narrative to explore the complicated and multifaceted perspectives black women face in contemporary society. The women in her book join her in an open and honest dialogue to help each other navigate new sexual paths that are decidedly different from the conduits their mothers traveled.

The memoir is a powerful genre for female sexual expression. *I, Tina: My Life Story* reveals intimate stories from sultry music legend Tina Turner, like her first sexual experience in the backseat of a car as well as disturbing sexual encounters with former husband Ike Turner. Janice Dickinson (2002), Pamela Des Barres (2005), and Jane Fonda (2006) provide us with sexy portrayals of the worlds of high fashion modeling, rock and roll, and Hollywood.

More recently, Carmen Bryan explores the contemporary world of sex and hip-hop in her memoir *It's No Secret*. She documents her love triangle with two of hip-hop's premier living legends, Nas and Jay-Z, as well as sexual liaisons with basketball superstar Allen Iverson. She discloses intimate details like her first sexual encounter with Nas:

> His manhood stood erect. His size was average, but that didn't diminish my desire to jump on him . . . As soon as I was centered, Nas immediately started thrusting inside of me. I told him to be still, then took my time riding him . . . Our gentle lovemaking turned into pure, hot, passionate sex. (Bryan 2006: 53)

Bryan describes Allen Iverson as a lean and muscled warrior with a scrumptious body, intoxicating kiss, great physical strength to shift her body into erotic positions, and a penis with normal size but exceptional girth and technique. She depicts a softer side of Jay-Z as warm and humble, and discusses how the two sneak off on sexcapades for five years while she is dating Nas, a fact that eventually becomes public through the lyrics of Jay-Z's songs and ignites an explosive battle between the two rappers. Carmen's vivid descriptions of the physical anatomy and sexual habits of powerful famous men expose how memoirs embolden women with the rare opportunity to objectify men and control their sexual representation in pop culture.

While Carmen's book documents her role behind one of the greatest feuds in hip-hop history, no woman exposes the sexualized underworld of black celebrity life quite like a former video vixen named Karrine Steffans. After several years of dancing scantily clad in hip-hop videos, co-starring in a major motion picture, and also appearing in a sex video, Karrine eventually documents her difficult childhood, battles with drug and alcohol addiction, and numerous trysts with artists, actors, and Hollywood power moguls. Her memoir, *Confessions of a Video Vixen*, hits the shelves in 2005 providing tantalizing details of her sexual adventures with powerful celebrities, while drawing harsh criticism from blogs and Internet chat rooms as quickly as it becomes a *New York Times* bestseller. Eventually selling around 500,000 copies, the book still strikes a chord in popular culture. Some perceive it as an empowering narrative for women, exposing the pitfalls of sexual exploitation and domestic violence. But many others see it as a self-serving ploy to punish her enemies and fatten her pocketbook.

Confessions of a Video Vixen documents Karrine's early childhood as a smart girl whose mother physically abuses her and whose father virtually ignores her. As a young teen, an older roughneck rapes her, and years later a disgruntled rapper abuses her verbally and physically in a tumultuous long-term relationship. She eventually conjures up the strength to abscond with her son to Los Angeles to start a new life. On a quest to gain love and acceptance, she becomes easy prey to the seductions of Hollywood including drugs, wild parties, and numerous sexual relations with celebrities. She hits several low points that inspire her to live a more proactive life and *Confessions* is a snapshot of the good, the bad, and the ugly facets that spawn her self-discovery. After *Confessions* she publishes two more books, *The Vixen Diaries*, a snapshot of her new life since becoming a celebrity, and *The Vixen Manual*, a virtual how-to on romance and sex. Both subsequent works enjoy considerable success but it is her initial memoir that catapults her into the pop-cultural stratosphere and defines her concurrent career as public provocateur, creating new spaces to discuss women and sexuality.

It is easy to envisage Karrine Steffans as the incarnation of Emma Bovary, the tragic heroine of Gustave Flaubert's nineteenth-century novel *Madam Bovary*. Emma cheats on her husband, disregards her child, and sends the family into financial collapse. Similarly, Karrine makes herself sexually available to gain entree among powerful men and neglects her child in pursuit of passion and power. Both women desire a certain beauty of life that their socioeconomic conditions cannot afford and both allow their longings to become self-destructive. Both women attempt suicide, but whereas Emma's life ends tragically, Karrine's life enters transformation. By age twenty-six, Karrine commodifies her story and becomes a best-selling author, finally enjoying the good life on her own terms. Why is it easier for people to sympathize with Emma Bovary than with the video vixen?

For one, Emma's suicide prevents the opportunity for her to reflect on her past associations with powerful suitors from a vantage point of power. Karrine, on the other hand, writes a bestseller that provides a pulpit in popular culture where her interpretations of her life and depictions of powerful men now matter. In a male-dominated society, such entrée as judge and jury of male sexual performance will inevitably engender resentment. Secondly,

Emma has a more acceptable position as a doctor's wife, whereas Karrine is a video dancer, one of the most degraded positions in the status hierarchy (a notch above a stripper). Additionally, Emma Bovary does not discuss the penis size of her conquests, nor does she brag about her sexual power to seduce men, hence she is a safer figure to endorse and romanticize. Karrine conversely is defiant and sassy, a walking conflagration against gendered systems of sexual inequality. To the chagrin of many correlates of the black bourgeoisie—the custodians of all that is good and tasteful for the progress of the black race—Karrine refuses to curb her tongue. The fact that Karrine emerges as a dominant figure without regard to institutional support or climbing up traditional channels of black leadership is an affront to the prevailing gatekeepers of good taste and racial uplift, the purveyors of black middle-class sensibilities. Karrine then circumvents the politics of respectability before morphing into a sensationalized persona in her own right: the woman many people love to scorn, the enigmatic video vixen who rigorously refuses to relent.

The sexualized aspect of Karrine's story and her corresponding feminist ramblings about sexual freedom ignite a vigorous exchange between former rapper-turned-noted-author Sister Souljah and myself during her visit to Tulane University in 2007. Souljah, like many feminists, journalists, and bloggers, maintains that the popularity of Karrine's memoir is almost entirely attributable to the decadence of American culture. In her keynote address, Souljah depicts Karrine as a corruptive force to black youth, and during our later quarrel she further contends that Karrine's continued instability is reflective of the fact that "she continues to degrade herself with illicit sexual behavior," alluding to her alleged ongoing affair with singer Bobby Brown among other aspects of her personal life. Souljah deduces that if Karrine's emotional health was truly sound, then she would live a more chaste life which included her denunciation of promiscuity and her refraining from intimate escapades with music superstars such as Usher. Many disgruntled posts on Internet blogs and chat rooms affirm Souljah's verdict that Karrine advocates a loose sexuality overwhelmingly harmful to young women. But a large part of such repulsing of Karrine's memoir has deep roots in traditional sexual scripts that reserve sexual exploration and subjectivity for men.

I use *Confessions of a Video Vixen* as a required text for my "Hip-hop and Urban Culture" course and I am struck by the venomous response of many students, in particular women, against Karrine. Her sexual adventures with rappers, actors, and athletes make many of the coeds irate, some deeming her little more than the classic Hollywood whore. Several women chastise Karrine's election to publicize her affairs with powerful men, exposing their secrets and indiscretions to the world. Other students refer to Karrine's starring role in the

Mr. Marcus and Superhead adult video to substantiate their branding of her as a ruthless opportunist.

In Karrine's defense, I ask my students why should she remain silent about her sexual resume when hip-hop artists incessantly brag about their sexual exploits as a matter of course? Did she sign a waiver before each sexual encounter stipulating her confidentiality? If she is writing a book about her life, is sex not a seminal part of her own story (pun intended)? I also remind my class that Karrine is an abandoned twenty-year-old mother, destitute and addicted to drugs when she performs in the infamous sex video (which porn star Mr. Marcus mass-produces and distributes over the Internet years later after she becomes a celebrity author).

During the first week of this course we watch hip-hop icon Tupac Shakur stand trial for being partially complicit in the rape of a woman, and listen to his boisterous rap about exploiting women for sexual favors. Interesting enough, none of Karrine's detractors express similar outrage or opposition against Tupac's imagery. In our discussions of Tupac, these same students display a remarkable ability to assess the slain rapper's shortcomings within the context of his life struggles while carefully considering the ambivalent layers of complexity that envelop his message and mission. In their overall appraisal, 'Pac deserves to remain a legendary figure in pop culture in spite of his accompanying frailties. Why, I wonder, don't my students offer Karrine a comparable dose of acute analysis and categorization? Why are they the moral police when it comes to Karrine's sexuality, while out to lunch regarding Tupac's rather reckless sexual activity? Where, I wonder, is the consideration of Karrine's turbulent childhood as the victim of parental neglect, teenage rape, and a recurring pattern of physical abuse in destructive relationships? The answer may reside in the fact that gendered scripts about sexual adventure ultimately lie beneath the passionate criticisms of Karrine and her narrative.

It has been noted that sexist thinking not only affects how men treat women, but also tends to distort women's relation to each other (hooks 1990). Surprisingly, the strongest and most vocal critics of Karrine in my courses as well as in much media discourse on Karrine are women. Many women are easily incitable when discussing Karrine's foibles, while men tend to critique Karrine in more measured tones. This is not to suggest that all women are sexually-repressed Karrine-haters, and that men do not play important roles in the stigmatization of sexually adventurous women. For men as well often disparage women who engage in the same sexual agency they enjoy, and some of my male students do express negative opinions of Karrine. The double standard itself reflects the residual effect of male domination. Yet, the fact that women respond to Karrine with a disproportionate level of rancor might have much to do with how society socializes men and women to perceive gender and sexuality.

In the aforementioned documentary, *Silence: In Search of Black Female Sexuality in America*, Tricia Rose alludes to structural pressures that restrict many black women from enjoying a fuller sexual self-expression in fear of being branded pejoratively. She further expounds:

> The other reason I believe women are silent is that they find that when they say something, it isn't understood; it's heard, but not understood. . . . So if a person talks about herself and her desires, she is afraid of being labeled a "ho" or being labeled loose or promiscuous.

Other interviewees in the documentary also touch upon the insidious sexual script that encourages men to explore erotic potentialities to their fullest extent without fear of reprisal or censure, while stipulating that women, especially black women, must pursue sexual saintliness to guard their reputations. Rose contends we need more black women talking publicly about their experiences, which is why she wrote her book *Longing to Tell: Black Women Talk about Sexuality and Intimacy*. Her work suggests that part of black women's struggle for sexual justice should include a feminist mandate that supplants gendered double standards and the politics of respectability that limit black women's sexual freedom.

We still live in a society that is liberal in granting space for men to explore and discuss sexual revelry, while bestowing upon women a tight leash concerning societal sanctions for lust and articulation of lust. As a result, Karrine's unbridled sexuality and audacious sexual discourse invariably generate contempt. It is one thing to have sex with lots of men, but to brag about it? Such action is still considered unacceptable for a woman, even if swanking sexual exploits is a normal and almost obligatory part of manhood. While such an egregious double standard delimits female sexual autonomy, women are often the chief purveyors of policing and punishing other women like Karrine, labeling them sluts, reducing their value to that of opportunists or rogue temptresses with few redeeming qualities.

A crucial device concerning how societies construct gender is social mythology, a collection of ideas about reality that generate strong emotions to validate our place in that reality (Riggs 2003). Reiterating the latter point through the analytic of scripting theory, we can say that societies offer sexual scripts that affect how we respond to gendered performances. In her book *Girlfighting: Betrayal and Rejection among Girls*, Lyn Mikel Brown explains how school life contributes to the fighting and betrayals girls experience in their relationships with other girls. Brown reveals that by the time they reach high school, the "good girls" learn to rail against the seductresses who mes-merize hormone-crazed boys with their tight jeans, short skirts, form-fitting tops, and low necklines.

Similarly, in her book *Slut!: Growing Up Female with a Bad Reputation*, Leora Tanenbaum explores the gendered double standard that allows girls to denigrate other girls as sluts when linked with rumors of sexual activity, while boys receive praise for their place in those very same rumors. Her in-depth interviews with former victims reveal that in nearly every case "girls either had engineered the ostracism themselves or were more hurtful than boys" (2000: 11). Tanenbaum refers back to her own teenage experience with peers stigmatizing her as a slut for sensual behavior with a popular boy:

> In fooling around with Andy, I had made a statement that being sexual was okay, that I felt comfortable with guys. Hesitantly discovering sex themselves, the girls were probably jealous that I felt free to act on my desires. Along with the boys, they felt entitled to comment on my sexuality, to maliciously mock me and try to make me feel subhuman. And the intimidation worked: I felt utterly humiliated. (2000: 18)

She adds that girls often spread rumors about other girls whom they envy or resent, and gives countless examples of girls bestowing antipathy upon other girls whom they perceive or brand as sexually active.

Aisha Tyler maintains that part of the reason why the "player-versus-slut" paradigm (which valorizes men for sexual activity while denigrating sexual women as sluts) refuses to die is that girls perpetuate it themselves. In her saucy memoir *Swerve: Reckless Observations of a Postmodern Girl*, Tyler comments: "We call other girls slutty, look them up and down, roll our eyes, suck our teeth. . . . We don't admire girls who get what they want—we envy them, or pity them, or, worse yet, we fear them" (2005: 18). Brown, Tanen-baum, and Tyler all confirm that a peculiar kind of female antagonism against sexually promiscuous women begins in youth when mothers, aunts, and teachers introduce scripts that admonish girls to be ladylike, sit with their legs closed, and avoid dressing like those "sluts" who put out. This antagonism escalates when young girls learn to punish other girls who exhibit a hint of proactive sensuality. Violating the bounds of traditional femininity and sexu-ality often leaves women lonely and vulnerable to attack (Vance 1992).

Lyn Brown's contention that boys perceive each other's sexual reputation differently jives well with my high school experience. I do not recall ever distinguishing enmity between "bad boys" who, on the surface, appear to be sexually active and "good boys" who appear to abstain. I only remember most guys doing everything they could to convince peers they were sexually active, encouraging each other to cherish as many conquests as they could while ridiculing the boys who could not get laid. No doubt, most male teens are far more likely to make up stories about their sexual prowess than to endorse moderation or abstinence, with no likely threat of being reputed with a derogatory label like "slut" intended to diminish their credibility.

The high school experience is a microcosm of how society socializes females with scripts to be sexually demure, and males to be adventurous and frisky. High school boys become men who are nonjudgmental about other men's sex lives, and indeed are often celebratory of those who are able to maintain multiple sexual partners. Even men who choose to remain monogamous often live vicariously through their promiscuous male counterparts. Conversely, as girls become women, the good girl vs. slut dichotomy takes on more sophisticated expressions. Women continue to police each other's clothes, style, and sexuality and contribute much to the stigmatization that follows the so-called sluts to adulthood. In light of such gender dynamics, it is easy to see why Karrine Steffans' memoir raises so many eyebrows. Reading about how she seduces Hollywood heartthrobs with her charm and sex appeal causes many women to relive their conditioned resentment against those so-called sluts in high school who break all the rules while exuding sensual energy.

Let's not let men off the hook. Men are powerful players in our society, which programs both sexes to have antipathy for promiscuous women. Though tantalizing television programs with sex-driven female characters like HBO's *Sex and the City,* Showtime's *Soul Food* and *The L Word,* along with WB's *Girlfriends* offer subversive scripts that avert pressure on women toward temperance, societal sanction for male sexual agency is obviously more prevalent. Aisha Tyler laments that in our so-called progressive day and age, it is acceptable for men and not women to go after what they want sexually. She ponders:

> Imagine a female version of James Bond, a woman who bedded tasty young things at whim, then discarded them for other, tastier, younger things with utter abandon. A woman who had sex with guys after knowing them for scarce seconds. . . . She wouldn't be seen as debonair and worldly, she'd be seen as slutty and other worldly. (2005: 15-16)

Tyler's poignant statement exposes the hypocrisy of how society validates sexual virulence displayed by James Bond, a man who is willing to bed anonymous "tools" half his age without a second thought, while rarely affording space for a female counterpart, and alludes to an important double standard about sex as a gendered moral discourse. When James Bond engages in a frisky sex life with rotating partners, sex is seen as part of Bond's makeup; conducted as effortlessly as the air he breathes. When a woman replicates such action, the sex acts consume the better part of her identity and function as character indictments. Tyler anticipates a day when women have the option if not the election to act like James Bond, and can chart their own sexual course without fear of recrimination or reprobation. She writes:

> I believe that we cannot be free until we have shed this old, lame paradigm about women being chaste and men being wanton. The idea is not that we all become wanton, without regard for our own physical and emotional health, indulging in urge and impulse with reckless abandon. The idea is that we should be entitled, as human beings, to be happy. We are entitled to be satisfied, whatever that word means to you. (2005: 20)

No African-American woman does more to expose and challenge this gendered double standard than Karrine Steffans.

After my trial run using *Confessions* in my course on hip-hop, I decide to use it again as required reading for my "African-American Feminist Thought" course. Once again, many of my female students display venomous responses against Karrine. In reply, I ask them to imagine that in place of Karrine's book, we are reading a memoir about a male student's spring break trip to California in which he brags about carousing at Hollywood parties, and describes sexcapades with movie stars like Halle Berry, singers like Jill Scott and Pink, and sexy athletes like Serena Williams and Gina Carano. I ask if they would project the same ridicule they unleash on Karrine and her frolicking throughout Hollywood onto this male college student for his similar antics. My students concede that they would not judge the male student as harshly, understanding that, given the opportunity to have sexual adventures with beautiful celebrity women, most young heterosexual men will proudly go for it without fear of scrutiny. So next I inquire as to why they label Karrine Steffans a "ho" for the exact actions most of them would condone if enacted by a young man under similar circumstances without social sanctions or inspection of such a man's overall worth?

The public's blithe branding of Karrine as the infamous slut while neglecting to stigmatize men for their unbridled sexual activity exposes a discursive strategy to suppress female sexuality. Labeling a woman a slut is a way of using sexual reputation as strategy of power to de-legitimize and stabilize female sexual agency. Kelly James writes:

> Double standards change meanings for sex partners regarding desire, acts, thoughts, and partners. If a girl is labeled a slut, her relationship to pleasure may change. Her sexual life may be stigmatized by others, altering her ability to feel pleasure during the act. (2006: 50)

James reveals that not only is the slut moniker a pungent force that makes women susceptible to trite dismissals, but it also potentially alters their sexual performance.

Many people discount *Confessions* on the sole basis of Karrine's sexualized reputation without giving her life and story a closer inspection, as the politics of respectability fuels a swift dismissal. The mere mention of Karrine's name in some quarters generates a knee-jerk reaction: "That ho!" Countless people in Internet chatrooms and blogs marshal all sorts of insults and outrage against Karrine for sleeping with so many industry men, while questioning if she will ever shake her sexualized reputation. Predictably, there is far less Internet activity censuring famous men like music mogul P. Diddy for having several baby mommas, or male music stars Ja Rule and Usher for serial-infidelity fueled by their admittedly insatiable sex drives.

When superstar athletes Magic Johnson and Dennis Rodman write memoirs in the 1990s detailing wild orgies and sexual activity that make Karrine's text look like a Pentecostal pamphlet, the public generally perceives the basketball stars as young men sowing their wild oats: again, the proverbial "boys will be boys" motif. Similarly, many male movie stars, athletes, and musicians undoubtedly sleep with more people than Karrine and yet few if any critics question whether their promiscuity will dent their reputations. Music stars DMX, Bobby Brown, and Irv Gotti, and basketball superstar Shaquille O'Neal are stepping out on their wives or serious girlfriends when they have ongoing sexual relations with Karrine and other women, yet there is scant public outcry against them. Irv Gotti's sexual infidelity is a recurring theme in his reality show on VH1 as the predominant factor that jeopardizes his marriage and divides his family, yet the public still brands him as talented producer rather than "ho."

Despite such stigmatization, Karrine nevertheless responds with enhanced awareness about sexual politics and sharpens her resolve to attack this gendered double standard. In her follow-up memoir *The Vixen Diaries*, Karrine underscores the hypocrisy she encounters during her visit on *The Tyra Banks Show*. Tyra criticizes Karrine for divulging private information about sex with celebrities in her book, while minutes later on the very same show, gushes over Dennis Rodman about his sexual exploits with Madonna and Carmen Electra. Karrine justly asks, "Why wasn't he bashed for dating celebrity women and displaying his private life?" (2007: 17). Karrine exposes similar hypocrisy she experiences during her interview with Donny Deutsch on his CNBC television show *The Big Idea*. Deutsch badgers her for exploiting celebrity men, while on the same episode venerates guest Hugh Hefner. In response to such perceived duplicity Karrine offers:

> In Donny's words, I was "exploiting" the men in my book, but Hugh was "the man." I've made a living, in part, by exposing and displaying men I have slept with. Hugh has made a fortune, in part, by exposing and displaying women, many of whom he has slept with, yet I am to be ashamed and Hefner is to be praised. Hey, Deutsch, what's the big idea? Hey, Deutsch, what's the big difference? (2007: 18)

Karrine describes this as the "double-stupid double standard" that she often has to stomach during her *Confessions* publicity tour, and contrasts this with the respect and dignity she experiences during her visit on *Oprah*. The fact that both Tyra Banks and Donny Deutsch seem oblivious to the blatant double standard of criticizing Karrine for what they venerate moments later from male guests, demonstrates the deep-rooted disposition of sexist sexual politics. Recognizing the taken-for-granted nature of this double standard, Karrine states:

> My father once said to me that the worst thing I ever did was to be born a girl, because if I were a man, the things I've done would be either celebrated or overlooked. It seems as though only a man can make sleeping around, dealing drugs, going to jail, being uneducated, and being shot nine times cool and enviable or even worth mimicking. (2007: 94)

In this passage, Karrine alludes to how sexual promiscuity, drug dealing, and being shot nine times is desirable and chic for men, to make a not-so-subtle jab at hip-hop luminary, 50 Cent. She draws attention to the fact that whereas 50 Cent's career soars to unimaginable heights after dealing drugs, enduring bullet wounds, and celebrating his sexual insatiability and power, she conversely is unable to disentangle herself from the scarlet cloth, simply for disclosing her sexual adventures.

In a society that often treats the sexually reticent woman as the idealized woman, Karrine is launching a crusade against gendered double standards to anyone who will listen despite the disrespect and often hostility she encounters from her hosts. During a guest appearance on the satellite radio show *The Foxxhole*, host Jamie Foxx asks her if it bothers her love interests that she has had so many penises inside of her. His question presupposes that there is something impure or displeasing about a vagina that hosts much sexual activity. It is unimaginable that Foxx would pose a comparable question to a male athlete or actor. Yet instead of recoiling, Karrine retorts that her vagina is still super tight, firm enough to snatch off condoms. A few minutes later she tells Foxx:

> There's a double standard where men can have sex with whomever the fuck they want to and as many times as they want to and they're pimps. . . . So at the end of the day ain't nobody better than me; just because you're a man doesn't mean that you can do the shit and I can't. . . . Most of the men I know are bigger whores than I've ever been.

In her September 2007 cover story for *King* magazine, the reporter asks if she is ready to settle down, and Karrine replies, "No I'm not looking for no fucking husband. . . . Why don't you ask whoever the hot new ballplayer is who just got drafted if he's looking for a wife?" Karrine offers similar sentiments in her 2007 *Essence.com* interview when the interviewer brings up the subject of marriage: "Society says women need to settle down, have kids, and get married. I don't follow those rules because I draw outside the lines. No one has this talk about men. Newsflash: You've been socialized wrong, and it's not right!" Later in the interview, Karrine deconstructs the "video-ho" distinction, suggesting that a dancer having sex with an artist is no different than a woman having sex with someone at her job. She argues that sexual attraction can happen in various contexts and that we should not stigmatize those dancers who choose to have sex with artists: "If she's fucking an artist at 8pm, then who is he fucking at 8pm? These men fuck more than the average woman and way more than the average man. . . . So who the fuck is a ho if we're both fucking each other?" Karrine's last comment points to the fatuity of brandishing video dancers as ho, while pardoning their male sexual partners-in-crime, so to speak. With her memoirs, book tours, magazine interviews, and media appearances, Karrine challenges sexual hypocrisy and exposes the many ways society gives men a free pass for sexual exploration while repudiating women for sexual agency.

Similar to how gendered double standards inadvertently taint people's perception of Karrine's memoir, another factor that stimulates antipathy resides in a misunderstanding of the complexity of the book's intended purpose. Is *Confessions* a cautionary tale? If so, then why does the text contain so much sex and gossip? Is it a tell-all book? If so, then why does Karrine repeatedly refer to her memoir as a book designed to help women learn from the pitfalls that ensnared her, "a warning to anyone aspiring to the kind of life I have led" (2005: xiv)? How, one might ask, can a cautionary tale embody so many layers of sensuality and sexual seduction? I contend that the seamless blend of caution and seduction is the key to understanding much of its criticism, as well as its dynamism.

Confessions of a Video Vixen situates a proactive and adventurous model of female sexuality that many critics feel violates the unstated rules of the cautionary tale aesthetic. The standard template for the cautionary tale typically proceeds as follows: "Though life dealt a bad hand it was my own actions that accelerated my demise. I made my own life more miserable. I bottomed out. Yet still I rise ever-apologetic for all my past sins, determined never to repeat such mistakes." Under such an assumption, Karrine should follow the rhythm of a linear moral story like the preacher Juanita Bynum's famous sermon, *No More Sheets*, which first discloses her past moral frailties, and then reveals how God empowers her to walk the straight and narrow path. In a linear moral narrative, the confessor shows nothing but shame for past sins and makes a clean break, providing a clear before-and-after cadence to the story. A tacit rule implicit in such conversion narratives (especially if female sexual transgressions are crucial to the narrative) is that the confessor not take pleasure in her past "sins" nor by any measure glorify that which once ensnared her. Whether it is a testimony in church, a sermon, or a movie, the confessor of a cautionary tale shows only remorse for past transgressions, while offering affirmative advice on how to be a healthy and whole person. The historical assumption of the narrative's end is that the confessor will go on to live a righteous and chaste life, fully aware of the disjunction between her current and former lives. Karrine, on the contrary, has the unpardonable audacity to relish select moments of her perceived moral weakness, nearly-boasting about some of her sexual liaisons, more or less delighting in her sensual power.

While Karrine expresses ambivalence about calling her memoir a tell-all due to her admission of intentionally omitting many of the juiciest details of her story, it is worth noting that the inside flap of the hardback aptly brands *Confessions* as "part tell-all, part cautionary tale." With this dual construction, Karrine combines two genres with potentially conflicting purposes. Unlike cautionary tales, authors design tell-all books to entice readers and awaken their sexual imaginations. Whereas cautionary tales moralize, tell-all books seduce and sensationalize. Because it is part tell-all, Karrine often celebrates her seductive skills and sometimes shows little remorse for adventures with the rich and powerful. Even when she expresses guilt and shame for delusional and irresponsible behavior, several pages later she can almost seamlessly revert back to tell-all mode and bask in the afterglow of a sexual triumph. Thus, the highly sexualized tell-all capacity of *Confessions* creates tension with the unspoken redemptive intentions of a moral tale in which we expect the confessor to abstain from relishing in past iniquities.

We see these dueling themes throughout the book. The cautionary part of *Confessions* warns women not to abuse drugs and alcohol, virtually breaking the cycle by which low self-esteem can lead them into potentially destructive situations, while the tell-all side of *Confessions* enthralls readers through lurid depictions of Karrine's wild sexual adventures with A-list Hollywood stars like Vin Diesel. The cautionary side of the book shows Karrine's vexation at placing herself in degrading positions and neglecting her child. The tell-all side discloses intimate details regarding the fetishes and anatomical extents of her celebrity conquests. The cautionary side of the book inspires young girls and women not to fall prey to sexual exploitation. The tell-all side romanticizes her rendezvous in the ultra-luxurious L 'Ermitage hotel in Beverly Hills. The cautionary side endows Karrine's story with a moral platform. The tell-all side makes Karrine's story a marketable commodity.

Karrine does not apologize for selling her sex stories to make a buck, but it is this tell-all angle that rather unwittingly expands the sexual imagination of her readers, providing sexual scripts that subvert the politics of respectability. While the sexualized dimensions of the book exasperate the bourgeois sensibilities of aforementioned critics like Sister Souljah, others like journalist and talk show host Shaun Robinson perceive the tell-all aspects as empowering for women because those juicy details sometimes articulate a vision of sexual agency and adventure. Robinson alludes to Karrine's proactive sexuality during her September 2007 visit on *The Foxxhole* radio show:

> I think a lot of women respect her and kind of admire her and wish they could be as open with their sexuality as Karrine has been—not just talking about having sex with multiple men but just talking about being as confident with themselves. And let's face it; there are probably a lot of women out there who would like to have some tips from her on how to do [sex] a little better.

Similarly, T. Denean Sharpley-Whiting, while critical, admits that Karrine's sexy story "resonates with a telling number of black women readers" (2007: 97).

While we should not overlook Karrine's cautionary warnings concerning how insatiable longings steer her toward regret and self-destruction, there is much we can glean from and vicariously partake in, regarding the thrill-seeking path she pursues preceding her demise. Karrine recounts more episodes of sexual bliss and excitement in the four years of Hollywood exploitation and pathology than most women may dream about experiencing in a lifetime. The feminist achievement of her text derives in large part from the viability of her sexual sagas to provide a veritable template toward a more audacious female sexual exploration.

Jane Gallop reveals, "I learned that desire, even desire unacted upon, can make you feel very powerful. And the space where I learned desire—where it filled me with energy and drive—I call feminism" (1997: 5). Likewise, *Confessions* is replete with instances in which Karrine thrives on the energy of engaging and seducing powerful celebrities. She captures the excitement of her early days in Los Angeles with hip-hop icon-turned-actor Ice T playing the role of her mentor, lover, and friend: "When we were together, I felt like a woman" (2005: 89). She relives the sexual energy of her first encounter with rock star Fred Durst, and recreates her Miami trip with rapper and MTV personality Xzibit, tagging the reader along on treks to A-list parties, great sex, and fun on the beach. She admits feeling powerful being the mistress of Shaquille O'Neal, one of the greatest basketball players and most recognizable athletes on the planet. To the chagrin of the black middle-class gatekeepers of virtue and understatement, Karrine no doubt comes across as a lustful woman who delights in her seductive power and sexual dynamism.

Karrine confesses to being enthralled by rapper Ja Rule's swagger and discusses their first sexual episode from the vantage point of supremacy: "I was powerful at this moment. I'd discovered something new—I had the power here" (2005: 97). She describes her time with Ja Rule as five days of sexual explosion, "He was in the same place I was—pure bliss" (ibid). She tells us how she eats him alive and how sex with the rap star energizes her. Karrine describes her encounters with music mogul Irv Gotti as like a boxing match in which two opponents compete to dominate each other sexually. She savors one occasion when her sexual powers cause Gotti to flee from the bed and lock himself in the bathroom to recover from stimulation overload. Yet she equitably recalls other instances when "he got the sexual upper hand, and I would lie in bed, curled into a ball, feeling completely spent" (2005: 147). One can almost imagine a vainglorious smile on Karrine's face while she revisits such erotic conquests with Gotti. For a woman, specifically a black woman, to be celebrating this kind of sexual vitality is doubly taboo—especially if her readers approach the text with expectations of a cautionary tale.

Thus, alongside Karrine's numerous reflections of regret are meditations of delight in the sheer pleasure and artistry of sex and her penchant for seducing men. While some may cite her exchanges with Ja Rule and Gotti as proof of her blanket promiscuity, there are surely others who, intrigued by Karrine's sexual confidence, become more curious about exploring new heights of sexual bliss in their own lives. How many women can claim that sex curls them up in bed feeling completely spent, or that they exhibit enough sexual power to force a partner to flee from their presence? A better question is how many women can brag of sleeping with celebrities they have fantasized about since they were teenagers? Despite her frailties and moments of weakness, Karrine's presentation of the black female self as a proactive, lustful, and erotically curious sexual agent is nonetheless a powerful attack against the politics of respectability.

The ambivalent ending of the memoir perplexes many readers who expect a sharper resolution. Rather than undergoing a religious-like conversion experience to commemorate her personal recovery, Karrine instead gets her freak on with R&B mega-superstar Usher, one of her previous lovers. Sister Souljah suggests the book's ending confirms that Karrine is not yet ready to tell her story until she purges herself from such carnal yearnings. Perhaps Sister Souljah should re-read her own powerful memoir, *No Disrespect*, to remember what she was like as a young vibrant woman in her early twenties—Karrine's age when she has intercourse with Usher at the end of *Confessions*. Moreover, how many young heterosexual men would refuse an invite from a beautiful pop superstar like Beyoncé Knowles for a night of passion? Not many I suppose. Why then should we expect Karrine to refuse Usher, an equally compelling sex symbol? Ultimately, it is Karrine herself who clarifies how her last tryst with Usher is compatible with her own personal transformation:

> The old Karrine might have been looking for love, for salvation, but the new Karrine saw the search for what it was. I wasn't there because I was lonely or looking for my next high—emotional or otherwise; I was here because, given our past history and the friendship I believed we shared, I felt free to be adventurous with [Usher]. (2005: 200)

Inherent in the above reflection is the realization that, however poignant Karrine's personal discovery and newfound strength, it does not mandate that she unilaterally become a Puritan. The "new Karrine" still likes to get her freak on from time to time, but only on her own terms as what she perceives as an empowered sexual subject. Those expecting the new Karrine to instantly embody the sexual persona of an elegant elder statesperson like Maya Angelou inevitably feel that *Confessions* does not fulfill its promise as cautionary tale.

Consequently, it is the book's cautionary tale assertions juxtaposed with the book's sense of sexual adventure, which disrupts many Karrine detractors. Yet, it is my contention that this unlikely duality deems the text an intriguing postmodern tome. There is something less ingenuous about a linear morality tale, which reduces one's experience to a simple before-and-after formula. Karrine's self-discovery is messier, more complex, and seems resultantly more human.

Karrine is forthright about neglecting her child and abusing drugs, while equally candid about her sexual longings and thirst for power. She explores the most intimate thoughts and feelings behind her actions and captures a full range of human emotions in such reflections. She reminds the world that women too crave sex and long for adventure. She takes pleasure in her prowess to make men surrender to her sexual power. In feminist acts of gender maneuvering, she objectifies her male partners, deliberates on their sexual anatomy and performances, hence rendering such men public objects of the female gaze (for a change). A virtual judge and jury, Karrine applauds the energy and sexual artistry of Ice T. and Ja Rule, challenges the heterosexuality of music icon P. Diddy, and chides the penis size of world-renowned basketball superstar Shaquille O'Neal. Through intricate layers of transparency, Karrine provides us with something more daring and sexy than what a mere cautionary tale could likely confer.

When male stars award female groupies crass yet compelling opportunities to bask in the allure of celebrity life, muted female acquiescence often accompanies the reciprocal sexual favors such men solicit in return. Karrine, however, blows the whistle on celebrity privilege, or as Jamie Foxx claims on his radio show, "she holds men ransom with her pussy." While hip-hop artists routinely objectify women in lyrics and videos, it is rare that a vixen wields the power to objectify men and fiscally profit in the process. As an inadvertent consequence, Karrine's artifice will inevitably induce more rappers and movie stars to think twice about how they treat their female subjects in fear of appearing in the next tell-all tome.

Kate Millett (1970) informs us that sex and sexual perspectives do not exist in vacuums but are commensurate with society's cultural values and social habits concerning gender politics in general. Gender inequality in society trickles down to sexual politics in the form of sexual scripts that allocate safe spaces for men to brag about their sexual prowess but as of yet does not apportion equitable space for women to do the same without consequence. Karrine Steffans, then, demands her own space, a veritable room of her own. As such, the lazy branding of her as harlot is imprecise to the re-imagining of her as an assertive self-aware feminist who sparks women to confront their sexual longings rather than sweep them under the politics-of-respectability rug. She is an erotic revolutionary who almost single-handedly reshapes black sexual politics by inspiring fruitful discussion about female sexuality and mistreatment, deconstructing gendered double standards, valorizing female sexual empowerment, and arousing new scripts for female sexual artistry: all while guiding countless women toward a more proactive path of personal awareness and self-transcendence.

Chapter Four

Zane's Urban Erotica

Now is the time for the revolution! The female sexual revolution! As we embark on the new millennium it is time for all the real sexual divas to stand up and be counted. Embrace your freakiness. Come out of the closets. If your man can't handle it, trade his ass in for one who can.

—Zane

Urban erotica take on many different forms. Some are comprised of fiery female characters like Juicy Stanfield, a fearless nineteen-year-old whose unbridled sexuality leads her to dangerous predicaments in Noire's novel *G-Spot: An Urban Erotic Tale*. Others satirize gender, race, and religion as with Jill Nelson's *Sexual Healing*, which showcases two middle-aged best friends who create a thriving spa for black women to have their sexual needs met by attractive black men. Some are transformative, like Heather Hunter's gritty novel *Insatiable: The Rise of a Porn Star*, which charts Simone Young's self-reinvention after bouts with drugs and working in the adult entertainment industry. Others like Naija's *Between my Thighs*, Renee Luke's *Making Him Want It*, and Niobia Bryant's *Heated* are steamy romance novels. But the one thing urban erotica have in common is that they present black women as sensual, sexual beings.

With the increasing popularity of erotica it is surprising that few scholars have assessed their effect on black sexual politics. As part of a multi-million-dollar publishing industry, urban erotica create safe spaces for black female characters to explore lust and embark upon sexual experimentation. No black writer is more relevant to this genre than a best-selling forty-something preacher's daughter who, reluctant to divulge her real name, writes under the pseudonym Zane.

Zane believes it is good for women to be sensual and aware of their desires. She regrets that many women go through their entire lives without experiencing sexual gratification and believes her erotic fiction addresses that void by promoting "healthy, uninhibited, satisfying sexual experiences for women who are tired of disappointing sex" (2000: vii). In the introduction to her novel *The Sisters of APF*, she discusses the history of sex:

> In the beginning, there was sex. Boring passionless sex with women in the missionary position looking at the ceiling, wishing men would hurry up and bust a nut so they can get to sleep. That type of meaningless sex lasted for generations—from the days of the caveman, to the days of the covered wagons, to the days of the bouffant—men thinking they can get their jollies off and not give women pleasure in return. (2003b: xv)

Zane contends that since today's women enjoy more freedom in the workplace, politics, and other important spheres, the time is also ripe for them to take charge and stamp out sexual inhibitions and enliven their bedrooms.

Since 1998, few African-American authors have sold more books than Zane. Zane also runs her own publishing imprint, Strebor/Atria Books, which has dozens of authors and over sixty books on its roster. Securing a vast following through her books, Internet newsletters, and *Zane's Sex Chronicles*, a late-night erotic cable television show that reenacts sensual scenes from her short stories, Zane has become one of the most powerful black women in the entertainment industry.

Candice Jenkins (2007) contends that the contemporary publishing chasm between black literary and popular fiction indicates a real material wedge within African American culture. Consequently, we are lacking an acute analysis of Zane's canon. This is unfortunate because Zane arguably has more impact on black sexual politics than any other figure in contemporary American culture. Her books are more than just entertaining, they assail sexual inhibition and provoke sexual subjectivity and exploration. The multiple themes that shape and inform the dialogues, conflicts, and raunchy affairs in her novels provoke new ways of comprehending female sexuality. Because a thorough examination of her work is long overdue, I will identify and examine the salient themes that pervade her novels and short stories.

SEXUALIZED ENVIRONMENTS

A recurrent theme in Zane's fiction is that beneath the professional decorum of the corporate workplace or the sacred veneer of the church lie raw human passions that demand expressive release. In the Zane-ian lexicon, any setting can be sexualized. Zane's women then find themselves fantasizing about men or engaged in sexual activity in the most peculiar places, demonstrating how the potential for sexual energy is as ubiquitous as humanity itself.

In her novel *Skyscraper*, the corporation Wolfe Industries is a bastion of sexuality with executives and staff members lusting after and sleeping with each other. Chico, the young mailroom clerk, is sexually attracted to Diana and becomes boy-toy to Zetta Wolfe, the wife of company honcho Tomalis Wolfe. Zetta also has affairs with other staff members. Anastasia, a low-level employee, tries to seduce Tomalis into leaving his wife Zetta, telling her friend, "I wanted the dick and I was going to get the dick, the money, and the name" (2003c: 22). Bradford, a senior executive, throws penthouse parties to provide sexual favors for clients, makes unwanted sexual advances toward his assistant Diana, sleeps with Anastasia from time to time, and pays Anastasia to have sex with his clients. In *Skyscraper*, Zane presents the workplace as an asylum for lust, passion, sex, sexuality, sexual frustration, sexual exploitation, harassment, and even a place to find your mate, as in the case of Diana and Edmund.

Zane explores this sexualized environment theme in several short stories in *The Sex Chronicles: Shattering the Myth*. In "Lust in a Bus Depot" Simone runs into an old high school friend named Wendell in a bus station. After reminiscing about the good old days, Simone, hot and bothered, asks him if he wants to do a quickie. They seal off a public bathroom in the bus depot with a "closed for cleaning" sign and have intercourse. In yet another story, "Sock It to Me," Lou's Boxing Gym becomes the site of a steamy encounter when the narrator closes the gym at night so her uncle Lou can enjoy dinner with his wife. A six-foot 200-pound muscular patron named Geren Stevenson catches her eye, seduces her, and they soon commence passionate sex in the shower which culminates in the middle of the boxing ring.

In the short story "Body Chemistry 101," the narrator, a coed, confesses to lusting after Professor Mason since the first day of class. A few years later she becomes Dr. Mason's student assistant. One day, thinking about the professor makes her so hot that she needs some fast relief. She then locks the door of the chemistry lab and masturbates. Unexpectedly, the professor catches her in the act. Rather than excoriating the coed's indulgence, he initiates a tantalizing sexual encounter with her in the chemistry lab. Similarly, Crocket University is the setting in *Head Bangers* where a coed named Hope has an orgasm just looking at the school's new chief financial officer, later having sex with him in his office. Feminist scholar Jane Gallop believes the crusade to de-sexualize the academic environment is fated for failure and recalls how sex with two professors she reveres during college is an equalizing force in which she is able to make these men more vulnerable and dominate them for a change. She writes, "Lots of other smart, ambitious young women, many of them likewise feminist academics today, have felt powerful because they seduced their teachers," adding that sex with a professor can make a student feel compelling and sexy (1997: 43). Like Gallop, Zane does not present her coed protagonists as exploited victims of older powerful men, but rather as free moral agents who know what they want and appreciate their power to demystify professors and administrators through memorable sexual experiences.

Zane's second collection of short stories, *Gettin' Buck Wild: Sex Chronicles II,* also features the theme that all environments can be sexualized. In "Fuckastrated" the narrator lusts after her classmate while in "Penitentiary" Phoebe is a prison guard who has sex with an inmate to pass the time at work. In "The Subway—A Quickie," a couple returning from a show turn each other on in a subway before having impromptu sex on the train in front of spectators. "Damn, Sex While You Wash Your Drawers?" demonstrates that even the Laundromat is not safe, as two people spontaneously go at it on top of a washing machine. Jude, the alter ego of the protagonist in Zane's *Nervous*, has sex in the meat locker of a grocery store with a butcher, on the bank of the lake with a waiter, in a furniture store on a $2,700 bed with the store clerk, and in the back of a squad car with a police officer to barter against a speeding ticket.

Zane even presents the church pew as sexually charged. In her short story "The Barbershop," the narrator visits Bethel Baptist Church and sits next to her love interest. Things heat up when she nonchalantly rubs her thigh against his while listening to the sermon. Similarly, in the novel *Afterburn*, Rayne notices the drummer during a Sunday worship service, and does not wait until she leaves church to sexually fantasize about him. She later explains to a friend, "I know it was wrong, but I could envision him ripping my clothes off right there on the altar and wearing my coochie out. Sitting there in the pew, listening to the choir praise the Lord, I had an intense orgasm" (2005: 98). As a preacher's daughter, Zane spends much of her youth in church where we may infer she learns firsthand that even the worship experience is not devoid of sexualizing influences, and how floating in the minds of congregants are often unholy thoughts. Internet sexpert Alexyss Tylor lectures on how sexuality and spirituality are intricately intertwined. Similarly, Zane reminds us that human beings are sexual creators and that they therefore may impulsively sexualize any environment, even church.

WOMEN AS LUSTFUL AND SEXUALLY PROACTIVE

If Zane's characterizations depict that all localities can be sexualized, then her heroines are sensuous, lustful creatures. Many of her female protagonists break traditional scripts for femininity by fantasizing about the size and contours of male sexual anatomy and relegating men to the female gaze. Zane's women are lustful, visual, and sexually adventurous, often taking control of sexual interactions by overpowering their men. Her characters are often well-respected professional women with a great sense of style, suggesting that sophistication and sexuality can peacefully coexist.

Stories involving Alpha Phi Fuckem (APF), a secret sorority of professional black women with insatiable sexual appetites, are Zane's most overt attempts at challenging the notion that black women are sexually repressed, or that women in general are not innately as sexually fervent as men. APF first appears in two short stories in *The Sex Chronicles: Shattering the Myth*, and her fan response was so positive that Zane subsequently devotes two novels to the secret sorority: *The Sisters of APF* and *Head Bangers*. The sorors' exploits are so enthralling that fans continue to inundate her with emails and letters requesting information on how they can join the fictitious sorority.

APF sorors treat sex like art and men like disposable resources or "cum daddies," hunting them down for wild sexcapades and casually discarding men when satisfied. Local chapters meet monthly in secret locations to have outrageous sex parties and reconvene in a chosen city for their annual national convention. Concealing their identities from the select sampling of men they invite to wild orgies, sorors refer to each other with playful nicknames which signify their sexual proclivities: Soror "Deep Throat" masters the art of fellatio (as also does Soror Lick em Low); Soror "Sweet Walls" enjoys receiving oral sex; Soror "Cum Hard" has more orgasms than seem humanly possible; Soror "Dick Rider" revels in the exhilarative authority of being on top during intercourse; Soror "Unrestricted" savors sex in public places; and Soror "Three Input" is enamored with anal sex. Many of these sorors have boyfriends and husbands but don't feel conflicted about sneaking off to their sexcapades. As one such soror discusses, "There's no shame in our game. We are what we are. Sexually uninhibited women that like to get fucked right once a month. Hakim's my heart and soul but he doesn't fulfill all my physical needs so I get my jollies off elsewhere" (2003b: 177). Patricia, a soror for two years, discusses how fellow soror and mentor Olive taught her "the difference between love and sex and how both could exist in a woman's life without ever coinciding" (2003b: 70). This idea that love is not sex, sex is not love is another recurring motif in Zane's works. Though APF sorors have relentless sex drives, they are also thriving professional women, Zane's presumptive counter-script against the popular notion that frisky women lack credentials. (That one of the founding members of the sorority ultimately becomes a governor further underscores this point). By upholding their professional acumen, Zane sanctions female sexual aggression and exploration as authentically attached to black bourgeois values.

Most of Zane's short stories feature one or more black women with a voracious sex drive. Shameika Zales, the narrator in "Fuckastrated," likes to have
sex three times a day, while the narrator of "Down for Whatever" is a twenty-
three-year-old woman who, as the title suggests, is down for whatever. Similarly, the thirty-five-year-old narrator of "Gettin' Buck Wild" informs us of
her life-altering decision to openly engage in sex with numerous partners,
eventually starring in her first porno flick.

Zetta Wolfe, the lustful temptress in *Skyscraper*, reveals her erotic under-
pinnings to one of her suitors, "Chico, I knew from the first time that I had
sex that it was going to be an essential part of my life. Some women barely
enjoy sex; some of them never even cum, but not me. I live for it" (2003c:
164). "The Dick You Down Crew" is a short story about lonely women who
enliven their sex lives by hiring the services of a group of men committed to
giving women the ultimate sexual experience.

Many of Zane's women are not shy about lusting after male sexual
anatomy. In "The Voyeur" a happily married woman uses a telescope to
gaze at her male neighbor from across the avenue. Hope, a twin sister in
Head Bangers, claims, "I can't imagine life without dick" (2009: 20). In
Shame on It All, after her sisters catch her eyeing the bartender's penis,
Bryce reveals that women check men out too, everything from their shoes
to their fingernails to their nature. Later in the novel, Bryce, her sisters,
and friends visit a club called Black Screw and lust after male dancers clad
in G-strings and boots. Not long after arriving, the women vocalize their
fascination with Mandingo, a particularly well-endowed dancer. *The Heat
Seekers* has women from eighteen to eighty hankering after male exotic
dancers at a bachelorette party. In *Skyscraper*, Diana is not interested in
Edmund until she sees him moonlighting as an erotic dancer; she later discusses his performance: "Yes it made me horny. I'm a grown woman and
have teenage kids and I'm confident enough about my sexuality to be able
to say it" (2003c: 128).

Zane's female protagonists are daring enough to initiate sexual encounters
with men. In "Be My Valentine," while out on her first date with a male
companion, the narrator abruptly alerts him that, "I want you to take me some
place and fuck me in all three holes till I pass the hell out!" (2000: 23). They
then venture to the club's fire escape where she grabs his penis out his pants,
makes him receive oral pleasure, and then demands that the favor be returned.
In the abovementioned short story "Lust in a Bus Depot," it is Simone who
suggests they do a quickie in the bus depot, and in "Barbershop" the female
protagonist practically stalks her male interest until he finally relents to her
sexual onslaught one late night at the barbershop. In *Nervous*, Jude entices
her neighbor's boyfriend by standing on her balcony topless and dancing

seductively. Seconds later, he joins her for a nightcap only a few doors away from his girlfriend's apartment.

Sometimes Zane's women kick off sexual encounters with new suitors to punish cheating partners. In "Sweet Revenge," after the narrator's husband sleeps with her best friend she retaliates by seducing her best friend's husband. The protagonist of "A Night at the Movies" discovers that her boyfriend is cheating on her and returns the favor by seducing an attractive guy in the popcorn line and having sex with him during the movie. Likewise, the narrator in "The Godfather" suspects her husband Tyler is cheating so she fires up a sizzling affair with his best friend Norman.

But Zane's women do not always require provocation to cheat on their beaus. In *Afterburn*, Roxie is crazy enough to have sex with another man on her boyfriend's balcony at his own party! Not to be undone, Zetta Wolfe treats stepping outside of her marriage like a competitive sport in *Skyscraper*. In *The Sisters of APF*, Soror Patricia has a handful of sex partners on the side even though her boyfriend has recently proposed to her. In "Mailman" the naked narrator receives a package from her young mailman and then lures him inside for a sexcapade. Later that evening when her partner comes home and asks, "Did you have a productive day sweetheart?" she shamelessly replies, "Absolutely, very productive" (2000: 172). In *Dear G-Spot*, her only non-fiction book, Zane shares real-life testimonies of horny housewives and girlfriends engaging in risky affairs behind their partners' backs, including the email from a preacher's wife who ventures into the world of S&M with older, more experienced men. Zane's stories and real-life email correspondences insinuate wide-ranging factors behind women cheating, but they all center upon the theme of women as sexual creatures with strong desires that need fulfillment.

Women's acceptance of masturbation increases along with their desire for sexual equality (Schwartz and Rutter 1998). Zane portrays masturbation as an important device in the sexual toolkit of women, discrediting many of the myths while maintaining that self-pleasure should be *de rigueur*. While many black women view it as unnatural, Zane's protagonists enjoy masturbating, and are quite resourceful at maximizing its rewards. In *Addicted*, Zoë masturbates in her car with an umbrella and on other occasions uses dildos, vibrators, and kinky sex toys like Ben Wa balls to compensate for her disappointing sex life with her husband. In "Body Chemistry 101," the narrator gets so turned on thinking about Professor Mason that she uses a large test tube to masturbate in the chemistry lab. In *The Sisters of APF*, Mary Ann secretly catches Olive having sex with Drayton in an alley and masturbates while watching their performance. Even elderly women like Aunt Mabel and Janessa's grandmother use dildos and vibrators to satisfy their needs in *The*

Heat Seekers. As proactive sexual agents, Zane's women are proud of their masturbatory skills and often trade tips with cohorts on ways to enhance self-pleasure. Zane depicts self-pleasure as a natural aspect of human experience, an exciting prelude or postscript to a sexual encounter, a nice supplement to an exciting sex life, or a dependable substitute in the absence of a viable partner.

Another dimension to the lustful or sexually proactive theme concerning Zane's female protagonists is a fascination with oral sex. Her women are not shy about giving oral pleasure and their unabashed enjoyment deconstructs the stigma often attributed to this practice. In the short story "Cum for Me Boo," the narrator is a self-professed cum addict and sees sperm as a delicacy. During one encounter, she ties Brandon to a dining-room chair, rides him until he is about to climax and extracts the catalytic fluid from him orally. In the short story "Alpha Phi Fuckem" an ophthalmologist by day mutates into Soror "Deep Throat" by night, orally pleasing almost every male attendee at one of the sorority's national conventions. In the novel *The Sisters of APF*, Patricia admits that she can "suck a mean dick" but gives props to Soror Yvette who has it down to a science. In *Shame on It All*, Lucky brags to her older sisters about a recent sexual encounter: "To be frank, whenever I suck dick, it is never for the benefit of the brotha. Sucking dick is all about me. I love sucking some damn dick, and suck a damn dick I did. . . . His cum got me hooked. It was so damn delectable; I could drink that shit by the gallon" (2001: 63). In Head Bangers, Faith told her new boyfriend Kevin, "I could suck your dick for breakfast, lunch, and dinner. I could suck it for a midnight snack, to get rid of a toothache, to cure a headache. There is something magical about your dick" (2009: 39). Anastasia described Barron's cum as tart but good in *Skyscraper*; and women can purchase sperm shots in a club called Fetishes, which is featured in the short story "Valley of the Freaks." When offering oral sex, Zane's protagonists aren't just taking one for the team; they savor the power of having the penis under their control, and delight in the taste of semen, often comparing its taste to that of previous men.

Women in Zane's stories also celebrate the ecstasy of receiving oral plea-sure, and often demand it from their partners, as Hope professes in *Head Bangers*: "Ain't no man getting this pussy without eating it" (2009: 78). The short story "First Night" describes a couple's first sexual encounter, which the man starts with a long session of oral stimulation to her clitoris. In "The Barbershop" the narrator grabs the back of Keanu's head and pushes his tongue deep into her with so much force that she jokes about having his facial features indelibly sketched into her vagina lips. In *Addicted*, the exhilarat-ing feeling of receiving oral sex contributes to Zoë's penchant for reckless extra-marital affairs because her husband is not willing to service her in that capacity. Almost every novel and short story in Zane's canon includes at least one woman receiving, requesting, or demanding oral pleasure from a man, and while receiving, she often guides the encounter with feedback. As competent professional women who relish giving and receiving this form of sexual interaction, Zane's characters deconstruct stigmas and traditional scripts associated with oral sex.

As sexually aggressive women, many of Zane's women also love "riding dick," which means working their skills on top of their men during sexual intercourse. Lynne Segal contends that sexual positions and perspectives often shield men's fear of losing control of the encounter. She argues:

> The standard biological narrative of active penile prompting and passive vaginal receptivity as the paradigm for human sexual encounter thus serves above all to hide, as well as to create and sustain, the severe anxieties attaching to the penis, while also revealing men's fear of recognizing the existence of women's sexual agency—verbal, behavioral, or physiological. (1994: 221)

Similarly, Catherine Waldby reveals that in the theatre of sex, the choreography of sexual positions reveals much about sexual negotiations and powers, maintaining that what feminism really needs in order to subvert traditional negotiations and expectations is a "strap-on" to penetrate the male heterosexual's body (1995). Likewise, Zane believes that being on top and controlling the encounter is an empowering act that controverts the traditional perception of women as sexual receptacles. She discusses in *Dear G-Spot*:

> The term "missionary position" speaks volumes in the sense that it is saying that the men are not simply on top; they are in control. Thus, when some women even think about actually controlling a sexual encounter, they freak out. Women are firefighters, go defend our country in Iraq, birth ten kids, hold political offices, and are movie stars, but ask some of them to ride a dick and they will freak the hell out, as if you asked them to commit murder. (2007: 55)

Zane presents being on top as another important part of the sexual toolkit of proactive adventurous women. In *The Sisters of APF*, Patricia and Yvette have a contest on who can ride the best, and Mary Ann marvels at the power and intense pleasure she receives during her first sexual experience on top. The narrator of "Cum for Me Boo" discusses how she "rode his dick real good, like a wild horse galloping through the woods" (2002a: 234). Zane devotes an entire chapter to the cowgirl position in *Dear G-Spot* in which she discusses emails from women who feel very anxious about being on top, as well as practical tips on how to control the reins. Zane's work is replete with virtual guidelines for empowering women with options, as she maintains that being on top provides women with a great amount of control over their clitoral and vaginal stimulation, as well as the enlivening feeling they are dominating men.

It is important to note that Zane's adventurous characters and their penchants for exploratory sexual activity are instructive, but not always prescriptive. In *Dear G-Spot*, Zane admits that many of the peculiar predicaments her characters place themselves in are products of her imagination and sexual fantasies, adding her conviction that "the best relationships are monogamous loving relationships where two open-minded individuals constantly find new and innovative ways to pleasure one another" (2007: 175). Zane recognizes that her characters sometimes make risky choices and place themselves in dangerous predicaments that readers should not blindly emulate.

Notwithstanding some of their excesses, Zane's proactive and sexually audacious protagonists challenge traditional scripts about women and present black women as complex sexual beings with expansive ranges of needs and passions. More importantly, they inspire women to adopt an unmitigated vision of their sexuality as powerful, adventurous, and fun. So while the ethics of Zane's characters are not always intended for imitation, the passion, energy, courage, and creativity they exhibit toward sexual activity are always normative for women, even while pushing the ethics envelope from time to time.

THE RIGOR AND SKILL OF SEX DONE RIGHT

"The human sex act is a product of individual personalities, skills, and the scripts of our times" (Tiefer 1995: 73), hence sexual proficiency is socially constructed. Scripting theory envisages an orgasm as the outcome of both biological and social psychological factors (Gagnon and Simon 2003), and is mindful that the topic of women and orgasms has limited sources of social support (Laumann et al. 2000). Whereas women often gain knowledge of orgasms much later in life than men, and are less probable to have an orgasm in sexual activity (Schwartz and Rutter 1998), Zane's novels deploy sexual scripts in which the female orgasm is a prominent feature in almost every sex act. Herm Edwards, football analyst and former coach of the Kansas City Chiefs, has a famous motto: "You play to win the game!" In comparison, I can sum up Zane's mantra for women this way: You have sex to achieve the orgasm and after that, more orgasms!

Most of Zane's female protagonists are multi-orgasmic, not because of some random biological proclivity, but as the result of skillfully uninhibited sexual interplay. Zane's construction of sexual proficiency emphasizes teamwork, communication, imagination, and anatomical acumen. She demonstrates to readers that when sex is done right—with vigor, savvy, and experi-mentation—orgasms are the natural consequence. Zane's stories set a high bar for men and women; they challenge women to step up their expectations, and they provoke men to elevate their approach. Zane's fiction presents sex as an art or craft that people can enhance with effort and imagination.

The theme of elite sexual performance pervades her short story "First Night." The setting is a secluded bed and breakfast in Maine with a couple on the brink of having their first sexual encounter. Their rendezvous begins with many romantic gestures by the male protagonist, including placing an empty water bottle on the balcony to collect raindrops as a remembrance of their consummative night. The story continues with a blow-by-blow descrip-tion of sexual interplay, showing the patience and skill of both partners. The narrator describes the actions of her beau as both romantic and erotic, sensitive yet rough, while providing the perfect blend of force and sensitiv-ity needed to keep her passions on an upward spiral. She exclaims, "I cannot ever remember feeling more desire than at this moment" (2000: 5). He gives great attention to her clitoris during foreplay. She grinds her vagina onto his finger to control the clitoral stimulus and then rotates her vagina and buttocks on his face and tongue, a proactive participant in securing her own pleasure. Both partners are constantly shifting and exploring new positions. He sucks her toes while she caresses his penis. She provides fellatio, while he sucks on her throbbing clit. Their back-and-forth cadence reflects Zane's vision that great sex depends on teamwork, timing, and skill.

Other stories and novels depict the rigors and savvy of sex done right. In "Sock It to Me," after thirty minutes of sex in the shower, the female narra-tor and Geren continue to engage in various intricate positions in the locker room. At one point, Geren lifts the narrator's legs up in the air, wraps them around his neck and bends over slightly, bringing his tongue to her elevated vagina before inciting multiple orgasms. In *Skyscraper*, Zetta Wolfe gives Chico "the best hand job ever" as her sexual mastery controls him from al-most the start of their affair. "The Airport" presents an energetic and highly erotic threesome with the participants shifting positions and working together like a well-oiled machine.

Zane's characters are quite adept at using food, toys, and various household appliances to enhance the sexual experience. In "The Godfather" the narrator describes the night of her honeymoon when her husband Tyler licks her left breast all over, covers it with salt, squeezes lemon juice on her from the center of her breastbone down to her pubic hair, takes a shot of tequila, and then licks up all the lemon juice until he reaches the grand prize. In "Seduction" the narrator squeezes a few drops of honey on her breasts, feeds them to him one at a time, then squeezes honey over his penis and her vagina and backside then climbs on top of his face in a sixty-nine position where he sucks her clit while she licks the honey off of him. In "Fuckastrated" Shameika ties up her partner, leaves the bedroom, and returns with a feather duster and cordless hand massager as creative tools to stimulate his penis. In "Peaches" the narrator and her partner have steamy sex, pouring peaches with heavy syrup over each other and licking it off. In *Shame on It All*, Bryce gives Troy oral sex with Listerine in her mouth. Why Listerine? Zane explains in *Dear G-Spot* that Listerine in a woman's mouth enhances fellatio by creating a warming sensation. In the same book Zane reveals other tricks of the sex-trade in the chapters "How to Really Fuck a Man: The Bottom Line," and "How to Make Love to a Woman: Mind and Body."

Zane shows that sex is a beautiful thing when performed right, but the flip-side of this illustration is that unsatisfying sex generates female frustration. Zane's protagonists chide male partners for lazy, uninspired, selfish, uninventive, or incompetent performances; men who are too quick on the draw receive considerable ridicule. She presents sexual dissatisfaction as a big enough problem to induce female infidelity or prompt a woman to abandon the relationship altogether. In *Addicted*, Zoë's frustration with her husband's limited sexual skill-set is the impetus for an extra-marital affair with a prospective business client named Quinton. After her first two encounters with Quinton she recalls, "Finally getting fucked the right way twice in one week was one of the most stimulating events of my life" (1998: 154). Quinton takes her to levels of ecstasy she thought were unimaginable, including teaching her how to ride dick, as well as the 72-position, a derivative of the old 69-position "where three fingers are inserted in the ass for extended pleasure" (ibid). Zoë admits she will be less susceptible to straying if her husband satisfies her in bed.

Similarly, in the short story "A Time for Change" Bridget contemplates leaving Drake for one reason: "He didn't fuck me right" (2000: 99). For when they dated years ago, the narrator allowed Drake's romantic qualities and sincerity to overshadow his sexual deficiencies—a mistake she inevitably realizes on her wedding night, where the honeymoon sex is swift, effortless, and "boring as hell," as she describes it. Sex does not improve in the ensuing years of marriage. Reaching the precipice of disgust, Bridget confronts Drake with an ultimatum: step up or get out! Drake responds with an open mind and willingness to do whatever it takes to please his wife. They make a fruitful trip to a sex shop to purchase some toys and later engage in many nights of experimentation, which save their marriage. Zane demonstrates here that sexual dissatisfaction can be rectified with willing partners, communication, and a stronger effort for sensual inventiveness. She writes from the vantage point that everyone can enjoy an uninhibited sex life. She introduces female sexual scripts that inspire women to communicate dissatisfaction and assert themselves with ultimatums if necessary, a far cry from the passive and compliant female sexual archetype that pervades society.

In *The Sisters of APF*, Zane presents sexual liberation as a process. Mary Ann, a sexually inexperienced and diffident woman from South Dakota, is dissatisfied with three weeks of sex with her new boyfriend. Watching Olive and Drayton have wild passionate sex in an alley awakens Mary Ann's sexual imagination. The APF sorors take Mary Ann under their wing and invite her to join the secret sorority. Mary Ann wrestles with the decision to take this next step, until her aunt, a founding APF member, reassures her that there is nothing wrong with being a sexual explorer. Mary Ann's process is complete, she joins the sorority and transforms from repressed South Dakota girl to sexually adventurous Soror "Dick Rider." In the sequel *Head Bangers*, we see Mary Ann years later as a respected attorney on top of both her career as well as her sexual conquests at the APF national convention.

THE PAST AFFECTS THE PRESENT

Another important theme that permeates Zane's work is the idea that the past is always present, particularly where sexual repression and addiction are concerned. In light of the above discussion, it is not surprising that Zane portrays sexual repression as problematic. But while she is a staunch advocate of sexual liberation and selective indulgence, Zane also portrays sexual addiction as equally pathological. She lists the symptoms of someone suffering from sexual addiction in *Dear G-Spot*, comparing sex addicts with crack heads and gambling addicts—people who lose all sense of proportion and engage in reckless activity. She tells us that prioritizing sex over work, family, and responsibilities, masturbating three times a day, excessively watching porno, or engaging in dangerous or illegal behavior means you probably should seek immediate help.

Zane's novel *Addicted* explores the complex factors behind sexual addiction. The protagonist Zoë marries her childhood sweetheart Jason, a loving husband who is sexually repressed and inadequate in bed. Zoë has a thriving business as an art dealer, three children, a dream house, along with an insatiable sexual appetite which thrusts her into simultaneous extra-marital affairs with three people. Realizing the affairs are spiraling her life out of control, Zoë seeks help from a perceptive psychiatrist, Marcella Spencer, who eventually uncovers that her sexual addiction has roots in childhood trauma. Likewise, Dr. Spencer helps Jason confront early experiences that influence his sexual repression.

In *Nervous*, the sequel to *Addicted*, intermittent blackouts turn Jonquinette from a shy and sexually repressed young women to her alter ego Jude, a lustful aggressive self-proclaimed dick connoisseur who initiates sexcapades with random men all over the city. Dr. Spencer and a helpful colleague unravel how a terrible family secret in Jonquinette's past contributes to her split personality disorder. Zoë makes a cameo in *Nervous* and tells Jonquinette, "We often bury things in our minds. The human body is a very intricate thing, an amazing thing, and sometimes we are things and have done things we can't remember" (2003a: 251). Zoë, then, underscores Zane's contention that the past affects the present.

Addicted and *Nervous* present sexual repression and addiction as pathologies deeply rooted in the vicissitudes of one's past while utilizing Dr. Spencer to show that professional help can facilitate recovery. In her interview at the end of *Nervous*, Zane discusses how many African Americans perceive the necessity of therapy as a sign of weakness, and therefore often shun psychiatric care and counseling services available to them. Dr. Spencer's prominent role in the novel series is Zane's attempt to de-stigmatize psychiatric counseling, with the hope of encouraging more African Americans to confront their pasts and utilize professional resources that are available to them on their quest toward mental health.

MEN VS. WOMEN: SEXUAL VULNERABILITY

Zane believes that few activities make a person more vulnerable than sexual intercourse. She often presents sex as part of a battlefield that pits the agendas of men and women against each other, revealing the humiliation and victimization that often accompany sexual relationships. In *Afterburn*, Yardley vows at a young age to treat women with respect and compassion and to "never prey on them and think of them as nothing but pieces of ass," but soon realizes that "by deciding to be as gentle as a lamb, I was setting myself up to be prey" (2005: 20). His victimization continues when his girlfriend Roxy cheats on him at his own party with his buddy. In the same novel, Rayne loses her virginity to Ruiz hoping to become his girlfriend, though he is just using her for sex. Rayne recalls more past humiliation:

> Since the loss of my virginity, I'd been with numerous men; each time believing that the current selection would be "the one." The one who'd love me; the one who'd cherish me; the one who'd stand in my corner. Each of them would enter my life, full of promise that quickly turned into lies and betrayal. I tried dating young men my age—the ones who appeared mature—but they were only after one thing; my sex. Once they got it, they moved on to the next victim. (2005: 30)

In *Skyscraper*, Chico falls in love with Zetta, who treats him like a boy-toy and disgraces him by sexing his archenemy, Donald. In *Shame on It All*, Colette faces humiliation when her co-worker Lloyd explains to her that they are fucking, not dating, and that she is too uneducated to be his mate. In *Heat Seekers*, Janessa wants to be in a monogamous relationship, but Dvonte wants to continue exploring other options on the side. Dvonte eventually gets Janessa pregnant and initially wants nothing to do with her and the baby, showing how sex can lead to unintentional pregnancy and abandonment. In *The Sisters of APF*, after Patricia has sex with Trevor, he moves on to the next victim and she feels humiliated. A year later, Patricia has to watch Trevor date her friend Mary Ann. Zane's realism depicts the conflicting intentions and exploitation often embedded within sexual relationships.

Anthropologist Carole Vance reveals that "sexuality is simultaneously a domain of restriction, repression, and danger as well as a domain of exploration, pleasure, and agency" (1992: 1). Along with the ecstasy of sex, Zane also presents the costly and dangerous side. Sex can cause humiliating physical complications, as in *Shame on It All*, when Mandingo's penis gets stuck up in Colette's butt and she has to call her friends to help set her free. The same novel also demonstrates how sex can lead to extortion, when a powerful university dean threatens to sabotage Lucky's promising medical career if she puts an end to their affair. In *Skyscraper*, extra-marital activity eventually costs Zetta her marriage and leaves her broke after the divorce. Sex can generate sibling rivalry, as with twins who sleep with the same man in *Head Bangers*, and even lead to murder, as when Zoë's obsessed lover goes on a killing spree in *Addicted*. Zane warns us that sexual relationships can produce harrowing consequences where scorned lovers become dangerous individuals. Zane depicts sex as fascinating and terrifying: at once capable of producing extreme pleasure or irreparable harm.

THE SEXUALLY EXOTIC

Whereas mainstream society often marginalizes sexual underworlds (Rubin 1992), Zane presents underground erotic enclaves as fun, experimental, and invigorating, whilst at times shocking. Her protagonists find themselves in peculiar environments and meet bizarre people and explore curious fetishes. In *The Sisters of APF*, the sorors frequent a secret warehouse bursting with naked men and women engaging in wild public sexual activity. In *Shame on It All*, the Whitfield sisters encounter Raoul's Midget Breeding Farm, where patrons can rent out little persons who are scientifically engineered to have "Herculean, gigantesque, elephantine, mastodonic mammoth dicks" (2001: 188). Equally surreal is an underground galleria of erotic business establishments called The Valley, which Zane features in her short story "Valley of the Freaks." The Valley has a club called Fetishes that accommodates every sexual craze, including a couple of pregnant strippers on retainer to squirt a shot of breast milk for $20. Freedom Café is another establishment in The Valley; it serves everything from hamburgers seasoned with vagina juices, to chef salads tossed with cum dressing. Freakiness is not a pejorative term for Zane; she normalizes the sexually exotic, and her characters venture out to sexual utopias where they are free to explore fetishes. Women have free space to explore a wide range of erotic interests without fear of stigmatization.

FRIENDSHIP

Friendship is another important theme that infuses Zane's canon, as many of her protagonists have lifelong friends they deem closer to their hearts than family members. In *Afterburn*, Roxie threatens to dump Yardley if he ever comes between her and her friendship with Gina, adding that "men come and go, but female friends, true female friends are hard to come by" (2005: 109). In *The Heat Seekers*, Tempest and Janessa have been friends since junior high school, and the sacrifices they make for each other reflect their abiding love. In *Skyscraper*, Tomalis reproaches his wife for talking bad about his best friend Barron and reminds her: "Barron's family to me. He's all the family I have left. If Barron wants to move in here, he can. If he wants a job at Wolfe, he can be the Vice President. Barron's welcome to anything and everything I have" (2003c: 28).

In *Shame on It All*, the Whitfield sisters have best friends who are almost as dear to them as their siblings. Bryce talks about being friends with Colette until the day she dies, and they both help each other out of tight jams, as does Harmony for her best friend Fatima. For example, Fatima wants out of her marriage and needs proof of infidelity to secure a lucrative divorce, so she asks her best friend, "Harmony, will you fuck my husband for me?" (2001: 41). Harmony agrees and the two create the perfect plan for Harmony to seduce him and videotape the infidelity. The plan works without a hitch and Harmony later justifies her sexcapade as an act of pure love for her friend.

CONCLUSION

Sexuality is a strategic axis along which groups sketch moral restrictions (Fisher 2006). In response to sexist regimes and scripts that limit female sexual expression, Lynne Segal (1994) urges women to construct new narratives about sexuality that focuses on the woman's body and sexual pleasure. In this way, Zane is a feminist because her novels and short stories draw new moral boundaries and sexual scripts for female lust and sexual exploration. Her protagonists present a more complex vision of African-American women as sexually curious, adventurous, and proactive.

In less progressive sexual scripts, the man occupies the position as subject (active, controlling) and female as object (passive, controlled); men act, while women react in this patriarchal blueprint. In Zane's universe, women get their cues from newer, more subversive sexual scripts that allow women to be active agents, emphatic doers. Women have healthy sexual appetites, take risks, cheat, or enact revenge on unfaithful partners by initiating their own affairs. They purchase erotic toys from sex shops to help them enjoy masturbating. They feel empowered by going down on their men, and indulge in receiving oral pleasure. They enjoy sex on top of their men and show great sexual agency. They objectify men, have multiple partners, lust after male exotic dancers, and seduce unsuspecting victims. They often give their partners feedback during sex, assuming that men can't read their minds, as Zane often reminds her fans in ezines and email correspondence. Zane's female protagonists sleep with college professors, have orgasms in church, and shoot their own porn flicks, while simultaneously living normal lives as doctors, art dealers, med school students, and politicians. They are active sexual subjects who progress through various stages from sexually inexperienced and repressed to sexually courageous and highly developed.

Although society has norms and expectations concerning how civilized people should conduct themselves in various contexts, Zane's worlds present humans as sexually charged animals, lusting after and sleeping with each other. She demonstrates that it is unrealistic to think that co-workers are not susceptible to sexually harassing, seducing, and sleeping with each other, that professors are immune from desiring students under their tutelage, that female prison guards won't find themselves lusting after big muscular inmates under their supervision, or that women filling church pews are always devoid of sexual feelings for pastors, musicians, or other members. Zane reminds us that the potential for people to sexualize an environment is palpable, however far beneath the surface it may reside.

Zane's novels also present sex as an arena of conquest. They feature proactive women who take charge and make men their prey, as well as passive female victims who subject themselves to male control. Zane teaches both men and women that in this dangerous game called sex, naiveté often yields victimization. She illustrates how sex has the propensity to tap into primal aspects of our humanity, the results of which can range from exhilarating to humiliating to, as in the case of her novel *Addicted*, quite lethal.

A careful examination of her canon reveals that Zane is a writer with great imagination and social import. She creates well-developed characters, complex plotlines, and intriguing backdrops to deconstruct traditional or stereotypical representations of African-American women. To the politics of respectability, Zane says "Enough!" While societal forces pressure women to control their sexual presentations, Zane creates guilt-free zones where women can indulge in their lusts and rigorously pursue bodily pleasure. Born and raised as a preacher's kid, she is now an erotic revolutionary of the first order, richly enhancing the depth of black sexual discourse while offering discursive strategies for women to enjoy a fuller range of sexual exploration.

Chapter Five

Serena and the Power Chicks

There used to be two types of women on the big screen, moms and sex-pots. Now we have the power chick.

—Gabrielle Reece

Under Armour Performance airs a commercial that features young women displaying the rigors of their sports. One swings at a pitch, another kicks a soccer ball, and others pound their field hockey sticks displaying rhythm and solidarity. Coaches are pushing players, and players are motivating each other. The ultimate scene cuts to volleyball players in tiny spandex shorts walking toward the court with intense game faces; one young woman pumps her fist like Tiger Woods to hype her team up. This Under Armour Performance commercial showcases young sexy warriors getting ready for battle. I expect some feminists to view the two vignettes that feature sweaty female bodies in sports bras and tiny spandex shorts as exploitive and objectifying. I, on the other hand, perceive the commercial as an empowering tribute to the Title IX legacy that opens the door to new generations of female athletes.

Title IX spawns a new cohort of women who take it for granted that they can be strong and competitive: exactly how the commercial portrays them. Female bodybuilder and feminist scholar Leslie Heywood discusses how Title IX legislation facilitates the entry of millions of girls into sports, making athletics no longer the province of men:

The fighters who launched the second wave women's movement (to whom today's girrrl-jocks owe our lives) nailed an important victory. It was Title IX of the 1972 Amendments to the Educational Act, which mandated equal facilities and funding for women's sports in any educational program receiving federal dollars. So, if you thought that girliness was for aliens and had nothing to do with you, you went out for sports. (Haywood 2000: 201-02)

The Under Armour Performance commercial is an acknowledgment to Title IX because the commodified female athlete was virtually non-existent before this legislation.

My grandparents and parents are products of a time when most people associated strength, speed, competitiveness, and aggression with men and masculinity. Susan Cahn's *Coming on Strong: Gender and Sexuality in Twentieth Century Women's Sports* analyzes an earlier era when media depict world-class female athletes like Babe Didrikson and Althea Gibson as ill-bred brutes simply because they transcend prevailing vestiges of the Victorian aesthetic for women vis-à-vis feminine decorum. Such an era, Cahn notes, is a time when the mannish lesbian athlete archetype is the "bogey woman" of sports. Cahn further illustrates how, as African Americans and Soviet women dominate track and field during the cold war period, two symbols of mannishness—black women and Russian "amazons"—pervade the media and impede feminist attempts to overhaul the reputation of women in sports. Since there exists a legacy of stigmatization (by Europeans and Americans) of African Americans as aggressive, unrefined, fervent, physical, and thereby excluded from dominant ideals of womanhood, critics could easily interpret isolated incidents of success in sports as the inherent effect of their alleged proximity to nature, animals, and masculinity.

While it is racialized notions of gender and sexuality that once contributed to the stigmatization of female sports, it ironically enough is the emergence of black world-class athletes like Wilma Rudolph and Florence Griffith Joyner (affectionately known as Flo-Jo) that plants the anti-stereotypical seeds of removal. In 1960, Wilma Rudolph becomes the first American woman to win three Olympic gold medals in track and field in one year and the media subsequently tout her the "fastest woman on the planet." Her undeniable beauty and panache make it impossible to reduce the Olympic champion to a branding of brute masculinity. A few decades later during the 1988 Olympics, Flo-Jo's ripped lean torso, colorful long fingernails, and flashy body suits unleash a style and verve that envisions the female athlete as both formidable and sexy. Flo-Jo becomes a sports icon and opens the door for successive black Olympians like Gail Devers, Gwen Torrance, and Marion Jones to parlay their elite athletic achievements into Madison Avenue marketing cachet. By 2001, a *Vogue* magazine feature exposes Marion Jones' muscular body to a larger audience, hailing her as America's hero. A few years later Serena Williams becomes the first black athlete to pose in the *Sports Illustrated Swimsuit Edition*. Hence, black female athletes have become prominent pitch-women in this novel era of commercial media ubiquity.

With Title IX legislation as an important catalyst to get more women into sports, the reinvention of the female athletic presence as competent, strong yet sexy, and imminently affable is a construction forging itself against the backdrop of cultural transformations that culminate in the nascent age of the "power chick." Fifty years ago commercialized images of sweaty young women exposing muscle tone and athletic skill akin to the Under Armour Performance commercial would seem strange to viewers of the day, unaccustomed to the image of the sexy female athlete as marketable archetype. American culture ultimately develops a new appreciation of strong athletic women as sex symbols when television and movies elucidate new images of female power beginning in the 1970s and peaking in the late 1990s.

Pam Grier flexes serious strength and flaunts effortless beauty as a sexy vigilante in *Foxy Brown*. Beautiful women overpower and overwhelm men in television shows like *Wonder Woman, The Bionic Woman,* and more recently *La Femme Nikita, Xena: Warrior Princess*, and *Buffy the Vampire Slayer*. Tall and muscular divas like Brigitte Nielson in *Red Sonja* and Grace Jones in *Conan the Destroyer* display "a sexualized female image which emphasizes physical strength and stature" (Tasker 1993: 14). Uma Thurman, Vivica A. Fox, Daryl Hannah, and Lucy Lui fight to the death in *Kill Bill*, demonstrating the deadly female assassin as a new Hollywood archetype. The acrobatic, smart, sexy, and extremely violent action hero Aeon Flux infiltrates enemy strongholds in the MTV animated series and the subsequent live action movie. Feature films such as *Girlfight, Crouching Tiger Hidden Dragon,* and *Lara Croft* showcase strong sexy women kicking serious ass. Angela Bassett's ripped body sashays across the stage as Tina Turner in *What's Love Got to Do with It*; and as one feminist observer notices, "Angela Bassett may spend most of *Waiting to Exhale* dissolving in tears and scotch, but her muscle tone makes her appearance anything but fragile" (Wurtzel 1998: 13). Demi Moore's buffed torso does one-armed push-ups in *G.I. Jane* as an amazing display of power and beauty.

Yoga and pilates training help reconfigure Madonna's body, adding to the legitimatization of female muscle as chic and sexy. Janet Jackson hits the weights, which shortly after yields six-pack abs and athletic muscle tone. As the twenty-first century unfolds, world-class athletes like gold medallist figure skater Katarina Witt, Olympic high jumper Amy Acuff, professional boxer Mia St. John, along with WWE wrestlers Chyna and Candice Michelle pose for Playboy magazine, carving out new space for sexualized images of power chicks. Mixed Martial Arts fighter Gina Carano emerges as the new face of the sport as much for her beauty and sex appeal as for her fighting prowess, toughness, and unrelenting devotion to the rigors of combat.

Madison Avenue too plays a prominent role in reinventing the American female athlete as both sexy and valiant. Leslie Heywood and Shari Dworkin contend that the emergence of the athletic muscular woman as appealing co-incides with corporate America's attempt to expand market share:

> In the early 1990s given pressure to diversify and conquer the "women's market," corporate America stepped in to fill that void, giving us extremely positive, even heroic images of women in ads for everything imaginable, and a way to publicly proclaim our identity as athletes—athleticism as fashion. (2003: 2)

Strong athletes like track star Marion Jones, volleyball star Gabrielle Reece, and basketball player Sheryl Swoopes begin to appear in various commercials. Women from the 1999 World Cup-winning American soccer team become cultural icons, as images of Brandi Chastain running in her sports bra in celebration of her team's victory and Mia Hamm competing with Michael Jordan in sports competitions in a Gatorade commercial signify a new age of the "jock chic" (Heywood 2000).

Few African-American women symbolize the dualism of power and sex appeal in this burgeoning age of the sexy female athlete like Laila Ali, the boxing champ and sports diva. In 1996 an eighteen-year-old Laila is running her own beauty salon when she sees female boxing pioneer Christy Martin fight on television on the undercard of a Mike Tyson match. Laila watches these women engage in fisticuffs and then decides that with her natural fighting instincts and marketable last name, she could distinguish herself in boxing. She enters the pro-ranks with no amateur boxing experience and trains three hours a day to get in shape for her first match in 1999.

As expected, the Ali name draws vast exposure and garners large earnings for each bout, which, along with marketing endorsements, allow Laila to train full time, a strategic advantage over her opponents who are forced to endure long hours of supplemental employment in order to support themselves. Moreover, there are few women in her nascent weight class who can handle the 5'10" athletic blend of speed and power. Laila's hard work pays off as she wins her first twenty-five fights and emerges both champ and ambassador of women's boxing.

Non-boxing fans learn more about Laila in 2007 when she competes on the popular television program *Dancing with the Stars*. Millions of Americans marvel at Laila's high cheekbones, perfect teeth, winning smile, and strong body each week, as she becomes one of the most spirited celebrities on the show. She brings the same grace and competitive energy to the dance floor that she exuded in the boxing ring. Moderators and judges repeatedly joke about Laila beating up her partner, and equally sensationalize her beauty and sexual energy. They construct images of Laila as both the cocky, strong, competitive fighter who will kick your ass, and the graceful, sexy, elegant dancer—an intriguing duality virtually unimaginable for female athletes just fifty years ago. Her ability to pull off both representations (powerful and sexy) demonstrates the dual motif of the power chick as strong yet beautiful.

Laila's popularity soars after her third-place finish on *Dancing with the Stars* and the dual motif of power and sex appeal pervades her media appearances. She turns up in sports magazines such as *Sports Illustrated* and *Muscular Development* featuring her athletic skill, as well as articles in *Essence, Jet, Vogue*, and *Cosmopolitan* celebrating her beauty and sensuality. Those who see her only as a sex object and doubt her boxing skills would be wise to watch her throw a right cross. Those unsure of her sexiness might think twice after watching her throw that right cross in a pair of Lycra shorts. Laila is the undoubted embodiment of third-wave feminist chic—we celebrate her skill and power; we marvel at her beauty and sex appeal.

Beyond the limited perception of power chicks as exploited victims, lie several factors that signify why they should be more appropriately celebrated as active agents and positive archetypes for women. Firstly, whereas we seldom see actresses and models without professional makeup and perfect hairdos, we often get to see sweaty female athletes in more realistic settings with little or no makeup and disheveled hair. In essence, we get glimpses of power chicks in their natural form as often as we see them cosmetically enhanced in commercials and print ads. In this way, power chicks provide us with more natural and realistic representations of female beauty and sex appeal.

Secondly, power chicks can be great role models by channeling the same leadership and courage they exhibit in sports into the arena of sexual politics. For example, WNBA basketball star Sheryl Swoopes is the first high-profile athlete in a team sport to announce her homosexuality while still active in her sport. The three-time Olympic Gold medallist, four-time WNBA champion, three-time MVP, and first female athlete to have a Nike shoe named after her tells ESPN Magazine in the fall of 2006 that she will no longer hide her feelings about the woman she loves. Sheryl appears on *Good Morning America* and in *The New York Times, Boston Globe, Houston Chronicle, Los Angeles Times,* and other media outlets discussing her decision to go public as a lesbian. Since coming out, Sheryl remains a cherished ambassador of women's sports and a courageous symbol for a more inclusive sexual politics.

Additionally, power chicks make great role models because the female athletic body offers a healthy contrast to the emaciated Hollywood starlet, a fact that is apparent when *ESPN The Magazine* devotes its October 2009 issue to the theme: "A celebration and Exploration of the Athletic Form." This issue features a spread of super-cut male athletes like NFL running back Adrian Peterson, NBA center Dwight Howard, Nascar driver Carl Edwards, and

Motocross rider "Scummy" Morrison, most of them posing in little more than briefs and shades. But equally compelling are the female bodies on display as essential paragons of strength and aesthetic appeal. Unlike the frail and passive posture embodied in most supermodel spreads, these athletic female bodies appear active and effectual, oozing with kinetic energy and sex appeal in every pose.

While some feminists might interpret ESPN's spread of sexualized female bodies as making women objects of the male gaze, a growing number of feminists see power chicks as sexual "subjects" rather than mere objects, aptly recognizing that women too are gazing at those chiseled female frames. Heywood and Dworkin (2003) discuss competing contingencies in terms of how feminists interpret female athletes baring flesh. One feminist camp approaches the media as pawns of an insidious capitalist patriarchy, maintaining that sexual images of female athletes reduce their strength by virtually encapsulating them as sex objects. Another camp, Heywood and Dworkin argue, perceives it as female athletes' "God-given, MTV-culture-driven right" to display pride in their bodies (2003:78). The women in the ESPN spread presumably fall into the second camp. Tri-athlete Sarah Reinertsen poses naked with legs and arms crossed in a sexy position, demonstrating a powerful body that we may infer weighs over fifty pounds more than the typical Hollywood starlet. Similarly, pro surfer Claire Bevilacqua flaunts the type of short muscular body you would be hard-pressed to peruse on the cover of *Cosmopolitan*. Posing in a thong, she clutches her surfboard in a confident, strong, sexy manner. Likewise Mixed Martial Arts fighter Gina Carano poses topless in red briefs with one leg in the air throwing a kick. USA softball player Jessica Mendoza appears in the spread while nine months pregnant. Such sexy snippets of strong female athletic bodies offer healthy media images of idealized women. Moreover, the fact that they're photographed alongside half-naked male counterparts demonstrates an equitable gender display of idealized athletic bodies.

Power chicks exude a confident swagger accompanied by a more proactive, healthy, and attainable image for women. To look like Laila Ali or Gina Carano, a woman has to eat lots of protein, drink plenty of liquids, and lift weights—activities that promote the overall health of her body—whereas to emulate the physical demeanor of most supermodels, a woman must starve herself to a skeletal frame thus demoting the overall health of her body. Even the slender tennis sex symbol Anna Kournikova has considerably more size and muscle than the prototypical runway queen or Hollywood starlet. Though female athletes have a long way to go before obliterating Hollywood's touchstone of the starving diva, the emergence of the power chick is a refreshing alternative to the standard media portrayal of feminine beauty and sex appeal.

It should be noted that no attempt here is made to project the sports world and muscle tone as panaceas for all gender disparities. For blatant inequalities still exist regarding male and female sports in America, vis-à-vis the way power brokers market such sports and images, as well as the opportunities particular athletes have to parlay their talents into saleable commodities. It is true that in comparison to their male counterparts, female athletes occupy a marginal space in sports culture and governance. Notwithstanding the work that lies ahead to achieve gender equity, the past twenty or thirty years have produced remarkable progress, as Nike, Reebok, Gatorade, and various other conglomerates now pay women athletes millions each year to endorse their products. Television and print media deluge the public with advertisements featuring competent and beautiful female athletes. Women's sports on a whole have made tremendous strides: Candace Parker is a bona fide basketball star, Laila Ali is a boxing icon, Gina Carano and Cris "Cyborg" Santos are main attractions in Mixed Martial Arts, and women's tennis is on equal par with men's in terms of appeal if not compensation. No other sport offers more hope that women's athletic events can compete in the marketplace than tennis.

One of the reasons women's tennis draws fan support and market share comparable to that of its male counterpart is that the sport has tremendous sex appeal; a fact that failed to escape the scrutiny of two leading sports journalists. During the lead up to the 2008 Women's Australian Open final, which featured the fourth-seeded Serbian Ana Ivanovic against fifth-seeded Russian Maria Sharapova, one of the hosts of the popular sports show *Pardon the Interruption* (*PTI*), Tony Kornheiser, breaks his discussion of the forthcoming battle to ask if it is okay to watch the match because "these babes are hot." To which his co-host, Michael Wilbon, abruptly replies:

> I'm not going to sit here and lie and act like the attractiveness of women tennis players does not count in terms of how much money they earn off and on the court. I bring you a Ms. Kournikova who never won, but who made a trillion dollars. By the way, you got that photo down at that *PTI* desk of yours of you and Serena that you're awfully proud of. What, Serena's off-court income wasn't in part because of her attractiveness?

Kornheiser does not disagree with his co-host, while adding:

> Honestly, let's not limit this to women. This is why Brad Pitt stars in movies and I don't. Part of Tom Brady's allure, Brett Favre's allure is that they're great-looking guys. This is how the world works; this is marketing and women's sports are hoping for women who are beautiful and competent and draw in the widest possible viewership!

Wilbon and Kornheiser remind us that sports, like entertainment, exists in a competitive marketplace where sex appeal is a vital and legitimate means of attracting fan support for both men and women.

Few will deny that a women's tennis match allows fans to see highly skilled warriors compete. These world-class athletes train for years to get their tennis game to elite levels and their bodies functioning like finely tuned machines. Tangential to the competitive performance, women tennis players often wear sexy outfits such as short skirts and fitted tops, which allow fans to delight in the aesthetic pleasure of seeing gorgeous ripped bodies as they run and dive across the court. Given the visual affection for women's tennis, one wonders whether the WNBA might consider taking a page from women's tennis by trading in those unflattering baggy uniforms for more sleek, form-fitting outfits which accentuate their beautifully toned athletic bodies. It might be argued that such attention to aesthetic detail would likely allow women's basketball to give the NBA a run for its money as well. Being beautiful and sexy and being taken seriously as elite athletes is not a zero-sum game.

My appreciation for the juxtaposition of sex appeal and heroic capacity inherent in women's tennis only magnifies during the 2007 Australian Open Final. This grand slam event sets the stage for Serena Williams and Maria Sharapova to compete in a dream match. Maria emerged to stardom two years earlier during the 2004 Wimbledon Final when she defeated then number-one-ranked Serena in straight sets. Serena beats Maria a year later in the 2005 Australian Open Finals. The burgeoning rivalry cools off while Serena endures a series of injuries, leaving Maria on top of the women's circuit. Two years pass and Maria is now defending her top rank against the re-emerging Serena. Just as few pundits gave Maria a chance to win the Wimbledon Final three years earlier, most consider Serena a long shot to pull off the upset in the 2007 Australian Open Final.

There is an equally compelling storyline in how both women defy tremendous odds on their journeys to the professional ranks. Maria is born in Siberia and her dad brings her to Florida when she is nine with neither money nor connections to the tennis establishment. Serena hones her skills on the public courts of gang-infested Compton, California before moving to Florida for more formal instruction. Both women ultimately sign lucrative endorsement deals, win major titles, and earn number-one rankings. Both are big hitters with vicious service games, who belt out loud primal wails with each swing. Both women are sex symbols: Maria as a tall, lean, white blond with an athletic-looking fashion-model figure, Serena as a black curvaceous competitor with hip-hop-video sex appeal. Maria embodies an athletic version of the good ole American blond, while Serena's fuller proportions are more subversive to Hollywood's aesthetics, even despite the large contingency of Americans who judge her curves as no less appealing.

Though they reflect different races, cultures, and body types, both women carve out similar spaces for themselves in pop culture as undeniably skilled athletes with unquestionable sex appeal. There is no doubt that our culture celebrates these women as objects of desire. But we also valorize Serena Williams and Maria Sharapova as aggressive, ambitious, and accomplished athletes with tremendous skill and mental toughness, traits we no longer solely impute to men. This 2007 Australian Open Final match-up then presents the world with a mélange of highly skilled athletic feats and visual beauty, which only adds to the excitement of watching women's tennis. At the end of the match, Serena raises her hands in victory after performing as close to perfection as an athlete can offer.

It is difficult to forget Serena's valiant performance a few months later in the 2007 Wimbledon Quarterfinals, when late in the second set she goes down with what appears to be either a severe muscle cramp or a muscle tear. Her father urges her not to continue due to what he fears might be a career-threatening injury. Reminiscent of basketball legend Willis Reed hobbling onto the court with a torn muscle in his right thigh in Game 7 of the 1970 NBA Finals, Serena refuses to quit, using powerful ground strokes and big serves to offset her impaired mobility. Continuing the match in pain, she limps, screams, weeps, crumbles to the ground, gets back up, and ultimately prevails.

Serena shows comparable grit in the 2010 Australian Open Semifinal match against the emergent Chinese star Na Li. Hobbled by multiple injuries, Serena has every reason to quit against the younger, perhaps hungrier Li who is representing the hopes and dreams of China as her country's first athlete to compete in the semifinals of a grand slam tennis match. Serena's mental toughness will not allow her to wilt despite the determined play of Li, and edges out a brilliant victory. After the match, ESPN commentator Mary Joe Fernandez sums up Serena's performance:

> Let's think about it, she's a winner. She showed it again in this tournament. You can never count her out. Coming back from a set and four-love yesterday, today not physically feeling one hundred percent, she just battles. She's got that will, that courage on the big stage in the big moment to come through!

Two days later, Serena grinds out an Australian Open Finals victory over the former top-ranked Belgium star Justine Henin to earn her twelfth grand slam, equaling tennis legend Billy Jean King's number of titles. Serena's great displays of tenacity remind the world that Serena is more than just a pretty face and sexy body; she is a fierce competitor and highly skilled athlete whose resounding zeal and resolve accompany her fundamental mastery.

Once again, reigning as the top-ranked tennis player at an age when most women decline, the twenty-eight-year-old power chick is a metaphor for third-wave feminist complexity. Serena is strong, muscular, mentally tough, cocky, fast, agile, intimidating, aggressive, and yet has also emerged as a sexy, fashion savvy, strikingly girlie media icon with pin-up girl propensities. As with Laila Ali's performances on *Dancing with the Stars*, the merging of female toughness and sex appeal represents the triumph of women in sports and a new day in America: Serena as sexual object and skilled subject. Or better yet, Serena as sexual object and sexual subject. Isn't this the same way we view male athletic icons like Michael Jordan? Serena, like Jordan, is a blend of skill and sex appeal that sells on Madison Ave and puts people in bleachers. She fascinates people because she is skillful and beautiful. She paralyzes opponents with serves at blistering speeds and powerful returns; she tantalizes fans with vibrant cleavage and beautiful assets on display as she hits those serves and returns.

Serena designs her own sexy outfits to showcase her curves as an empowered subject who controls her own representation. *People* magazine's October 21, 2002 issue praises Serena as a fashion trendsetter and *Vogu Italia* features her as a fashion star in its January 2004 issue. She generates more fashion buzz after designing and modeling a new line of tennis outfits for Nike during the 2004 U.S. Open Tennis Championship. She sports her black studded tank top, matching denim jacket, and black knee-high boots in her first match of the Open, and a tiny miniskirt during her second-round match. Her most provocative design is her unveiling of the form-fitting black cat suit, which generates nationwide office-cooler conversation for weeks. Serena repeatedly competes on the tennis court wearing shirts with low necklines, which complement her cleavage.

A true diva, Serena gets her nails done before every match. She once told Oprah that she ignores articles written about her but glances at every picture to make sure she's looking good (Edmondson 2005). One day you'll catch her wearing braids with blond highlights, another day she's appearing in straightened black hair. Serena does photo shoots for *Vogue, Elle, Essence,* and *Vibe,* but her sexiest photo to date is part of her spread in the 2004 *Sports Illustrated Swimsuit Edition* where she stands at the stairs of a pool in a sizzling hot bikini parading a fit and curvy body that is worthy of envy. A close second is either her photo in the black see-through one-piece bathing suit in the same issue, or the shot in the white bikini in the 2003 *Sports Illustrated Swimsuit Edition.* Honorable mention goes to her poses for *ESPN The Magazine's* aforementioned spread in 2009 where she sports a black bikini with legs slightly spread and hand pulling on the bottom piece as if she's teasingly tempted to take it off. In all of these pictures Serena looks strong, fit, healthy, and sexy, a nice alternative to the emaciated pin-up girl.

In their autobiography *From the Hip: Ten Rules for Living, Loving and Winning*, the Williams sisters take turns discussing their lives while dispensing advice that exhibits the rugged individualism of the third-wave feminist era. The book teaches girls and women to think big, take practical steps toward positive change, work hard, take control of their environments, become master planners, have single-minded focus, and exert great energy toward transcending perceived limitations. The book also encourages girls and women to develop healthy relationships, have fun, be creative, always accept themselves, and carve out their own unique space. It provides tips on exercising, hair care, and saving money, and reveals past battles with self-image, past mistakes in relationships, and obstacles they had to overcome to accomplish monumental tasks. Serena reveals a period in her life when she wishes she was a bit slimmer and less muscular, but "at some point it just dawned on me that this is the body God gave me and I love and appreciate it no matter what. These days I am happy with who I am" (2005: 78). She urges her readers to stop accepting unattainable standards of beauty and to believe that real beauty comes from the inside.

Serena Williams is an excellent role model as a secure woman of the new millennium. While second wavers like tennis legends Billy Jean King and Chris Evert see her as too engaged with fashion, acting, modeling, and other non-tennis-related interests, third wavers overwhelmingly perceive her as the ultimate embodiment of the new feminist chic. Serena is both a jock and a pinup girl and sees no inherent problem maintaining both personas. She draws from a broad cultural toolkit and celebrates her individuality as a complex subject. She does not sit around waiting on male approval and refuses to conform to societal expectations. She builds on a multi-million-dollar empire by converting her athletic prowess and sexy persona into saleable commodities. You'll never catch Serena starving herself to fit Hollywood's ideal aesthetic—she aggressively defends her size and makes no apologies for showcasing her curves in the tightest outfits as a subversive act on the pristine Wimbledon courts. Serena Williams demands serious attention as a world-class athlete, shrewd businesswoman, talented designer, budding actress, and archetype of female empowerment. She is an erotic revolutionary who deconstructs Victorian notions of passive femininity with her seamless blend of strength, athleticism, and sex appeal.

Chapter Six

Vagina Power:
Alexyss Tylor and the Sexperts

It is time for us to graduate ladies into a new awareness into our consciousness about our bodies, our minds and our sacred vagina! Please stand up in Vagina Power.

—Alexyss Tylor

We'll never be rid of our shackles until we at least learn to masturbate.

—Jessica Holter

A growing number of black women offer sex advice on popular television talk shows, Internet websites, blogs, U-Tube videos, books, and magazines. A few of these so-called "sexperts" educate women on sexual health and anatomy. Others advise women on how to spice up their sex lives, achieve orgasms, satisfy their partners, and make more alert decisions with regard to the mating ritual. To some people, sexpertise requires heady theory and systematic study; for others it demands a certain degree of practical success in sexual matters. Whichever way one constructs sexpertise, black women who fear turning to parents or friends with questions about sex now have a bevy of experts to seek advice from to expand their sexual knowledge.

Gail Wyatt and Hilda Hutcherson have legitimacy as sexperts from formal education and rigorous study as practitioners and researchers. Gail Wyatt is a clinical psychologist, sex therapist, and professor in the Department of Psychiatry and Bio-behavioral Sciences at UCLA. She has five books and scores of journal articles on various aspects of sexuality, and offers commentary on popular television shows and magazines. Her book *Stolen Women: Reclaiming Our Sexuality, Taking Back Our Lives* builds

on hundreds of interviews with black women to chronicle how past oppression informs present perspectives and pathologies concerning black
female sexuality. She encourages black women to become self-aware and
proactive agents in all matters of sexuality including developing healthy
relationships, affirming female sexuality, and taking sexual responsibility
to protect themselves from sexually transmitted diseases. Her more recent
work, *No More Clueless Sex: Ten Secrets to a Sex Life that Works for Both
of You*, provides practical instruction on how to have a healthy sex life. The
book debunks false assumptions about orgasms, explains how accessories
can enhance erotic encounters, encourages open communication and honest
dialogue from partners about what pleases and turns them off during sex,
and even shows women how to find their G-spot.

Hilda Hutcherson is a practicing gynecologist and co-director of the New
York Center for Women's Sexual Health at Columbia University Medical
Center. She advises women in sexual matters on talk shows like *Oprah*, and
in her monthly columns for magazines like *Essence* and *Glamour*. Her books
What Your Mother Never Told You About Sex and its sequel *Pleasure: A
Woman's Guide to Getting the Sex You Want, Need, and Desire* provide candid discussions on human anatomy with explicit coaching on how to explore
the erogenous zones on the navel, thighs, buttocks, breasts, feet, and toes. She
shows women about how certain sexual positions work better with different
penis sizes, provides an unrestrained discussion on how the penis works as a
sex organ, and even advises women on proactive steps they can take to revive
a penis that has lost its erection during intercourse. She informs women who
have trouble climaxing that penis-in-vagina intercourse is not an effective
way for most women to achieve orgasm. She discusses how tastes, sounds,
and smells can supplement the sexual experience, and also offers women tips
on self-pleasuring with vibrators, various water games, and clitoral stimulation. Hutcherson contends that masturbation is an important step for women
in increasing their pleasure during sex and achieving orgasm, and encourages
women to masturbate in front of their partners. She also discusses oral sex
and provides numerous illustrations of men and women in various sex positions along with discussions on the mechanics of each position and how to
maximize pleasure.

Whereas Gail Wyatt and Hilda Hutcherson stake their authority on their
rigorous training, research, and institutional affiliation, LaDawn Black stands
on the power of homegrown wisdom and personal experience to function as a
sexpert. She hosts *The Love Zone*, Baltimore's leading overnight radio show
on 92Q, where she plays love songs and talks about sex with callers five
nights per week. She also writes guest columns for numerous magazines, and
thousands of women read her weekly blog entries.

LaDawn Black reaches her stride as sexpert when she writes *Let's Get It On: 15 Hot Tips and Tricks to Spice Up Your Sex Life*. She discusses the book's purpose in the introduction

> It is my hope that, after reading this book, you will own your sexuality and have the power to up the ante in pleasure and satisfaction for both yourself and your partner. Sex should be fun and freaky, and I am going to get you to the point where you stop dreaming about the ultimate sexual experience and actually go out and live it. (2007: 4)

She teaches how to maintain a sexual toolbox filled with products that include something lickable and sweet, a medium-sized vibrator, cuffs or a scarf, and a great sex guide. She urges women to be in command of their sexuality and to study the latest sexual techniques, trends and buzz words, as well as extracting feedback from their partners on what works and what doesn't. She reveals how to excite a man's hotspots, including tips on how to rub or lick the back of his leg, how to kiss and massage the crevice of his butt, and how to provide stimulating oral sex. She claims:

> Ladies, oral sex is no longer an option in most women's sexual menu—it is an entrée. . . . And in this case, the favor isn't simply a quick ball lick and tip kiss. It is really sucking, twisting, and playing with your man's cock to the point where he thinks nothing and no one in the world can get better than this. (2007: 46)

She adds that giving top-notch fellatio involves putting your back and much more into it.

LaDawn Black urges women to put their own sexual satisfaction first, to be sexually courageous and adventurous, and at times to even use men as objects to fulfill their sexual needs:

> I have a personal belief that is going to go against everything that your mom, your church, your girls, and society have told you. I am an advocate for "toy-boy" relationships. Every woman should have at least one relationship in her lifetime that is simply about the sexual hook-up and not about love, commitment, or deeper feelings. (2007: 62)

She provides intimate details in her sexual history, including the several toy-boys she exploits, nude pictures she poses for in publications and for personal use, sexual interludes she captures on video, and failed attempts to persuade her current beau to have a threesome by adding another man. She recommends for women to become more sexually aggressive and experimental:

Kinky sex is often the best sex! Forget missionary and doggy-style and famil-iarize yourself with the world of dominatrix (sexual domination), golden shower aficionado (turned on by urination) and walking the dog (sex in the park with strangers). (2007: 90)

Similarly, she tells women who hunger for a wild lover to lure their sexually reserved men over to the "dark side" with a little "liquid courage" and to use their own buzz from alcohol to rest inhibitions, give a private peep show, have backyard sex, and really get on with experiencing life. She presses women to make their bedroom a place of relaxation and sexual play and get rid of the television, animal prints, and anything furry and cuddly that detracts from passion, so men will perceive the room as a sexual oasis. LaDawn Black's advice in books, blog entries, and on her popular radio show introduces subversive sexual scripts against traditional perceptions of female sexuality. In all her prescriptions, she urges women to be proactive agents in fulfilling sexual pleasure, and drives women toward owning their sexuality.

"Ms. T" is another sexpert who boasts of no degrees in her specialty; she stands on the power of her experience as a woman who has been very suc-cessful with men. Little is known about her identity, except for what she reveals in the introduction of her popular book *The Guide to Becoming the Sensuous Black Woman: And Drive Your Man Wild In and Out of Bed*. She is a black woman in her forties whose friends and colleagues bombard her for advice about men. The book offers a proactive brand of female sexual and sensual empowerment that includes tips for women on how to make their vaginas tasty (for when their men go down on them) and tight (so when their partners return from their trips, they will never know their women were naughty). She counsels women to be self-confident and not to focus on their so-called flaws: "Sagging breasts? Yeah gravity is a bitch. But that's why God made push-up bras, dearie" (2006: 32). She emphasizes that attitude is requisite for sexiness and therefore advises women to wear sexy lingerie on dates to feel sexy all night.

"Ms. T" helps women educate themselves on orgasms, including tips about clitoral stimulation, G-spot stimulation, female ejaculation, and vagi-nal intercourse, and provides a special section on mastering oral sex. She also instructs women on proactive measures to increase their own sexual satisfaction like doing Kegel exercises to strengthen their pubococcygeus (PC) muscle, which supports the pelvic organs. She claims that a stronger PC muscle can heighten the sensitivity of a woman's vagina and help her pull and squeeze her partner's penis better, leading to quicker and better orgasms for both participants. Notice the emphasis is on how women can achieve the ultimate sexual experience. Like other sexperts, she believes every woman should indulge in a healthy regimen of masturbation and shows women how to create a mood for sex with clothes, music, and scented candles. In her discussion of pheromones, which she defines as natural chemicals produced by living organisms that affect other members of the same species, she offers an intriguing sex tip:

> Before your man comes over for your arranged tryst, bathe yourself thoroughly with scented oils and bath beads, then just after you towel yourself off and before you get dressed, stick your finger inside your vagina and then dab the vaginal juice behind your ears, on your wrists, and the base of your throat; just as you would perfume. Take my word for it . . . it works! (2006: 88)

"Ms. T's" book offers an edgy and expansive dialogue on how black women can become more sexually empowered and satisfied.

Of all the sexperts on the scene, perhaps none is as unforgettable as an Atlanta native named Alexyss Tylor. Whereas the aforementioned sexperts gain notoriety through traditional means like radio and television programs, magazine columns, or books, Alexyss Tylor achieves popularity on the Internet. In 2007, she hosts her own public-access talk show called *Vagina Power* for almost the entire year, where she provides graphic viewpoints on the power of sex. The show is canceled after station management and a contingency of black women, purveyors of the politics of respectability, raise objections against her raw teachings. She now draws a mounting following by posting various video clips from the show (ranging from two to ten minutes each) on YouTube. The video clips help her gain a new following and emerge as a lecturer and provocateur. Her popularity demonstrates how Internet technologies can contribute to the democratization of expertise and produce new kinds of public intellectuals and celebrities.

In her June 2008 lecture at Spelman College, she tells students that she can identify with the struggles and pain of many black women because she is the product of a rape, comes from the ghetto, raises a son as a single mother, and endures many of the pitfalls and struggles that come from a lack of sexual consciousness during much of her adult life. The rigors of her experiences, the quirkiness of her personality, and her prescient comedic timing all come together to fashion Alexyss Tylor with a brisk clarity and ingenuity in bestowing sex advice. Though she lacks traditional education and training, her homespun wisdom and down-home vernacular provide a unique analysis on sexual matters, as she discusses in her most popular video clip "Vagina Power":

> I may not have any PhDs and master's degrees to put on my wall in academia, but I have a master's degree in being played by men, used by men, told everything I want to hear to get me in positions.

Alexyss magnetizes her listeners with fiery straight talk on sexual matters and her musings are often the topic of discussions on college campuses, Internet chatrooms, blogs, and websites.

Alexyss is defiant. In 2008 after hackers take over her YouTube account and websites and attempt to destroy all her videos, causing a brief hiatus on the Internet, Alexyss reemerges in a new video puffing a cigar, claiming victory over her detractors, and boasting that the Vagina Power movement lives on. One blogger describes her as put together on the outside, unraveling within, and another calls her video "Vagina Power" the best ten-minute short play ever written. Her videos use performance art and shtick to keep her audience's attention. For example, to commemorate Halloween she records her talk show dressed in a black pilot suit and begins the session with a charge to her women viewers: "Salute the Vagina!"

Her delivery is organic and penetrating, as she rarely cracks a smile while warning women against being "sabotaged by the dick," and keeps a very stern demeanor while she is discharging offbeat expressions like "a man's life force is in his nuts." Her mother is her sidekick in earlier videos, asking her daughter about such things as Jackrabbit vibrators and G-spots. Consider the ironic hilarity of her matronly mammy-like Christian mother proclaiming she's going to stay "prayed up" to protect herself from the temptations of penis power.

Alexyss offers provocative prose and bellicose rants that are much about educating women on the power of male genitalia to seduce and destroy their lives. The basic theme that permeates her YouTube video clips is that a woman is a spiritual being and the most powerful creature on the planet, but if men victimize, humiliate, and maim her on any level it begins in the "mind" of the woman's vagina. She blends ideas from New Thought teachings and Eastern spirituality to explain how a kind of spiritual homeostasis exists when women stand in "vagina power," or in other words, engage in the positive energy of healthy friendships and symbiotic sexual relations. She presents the vagina as the fulcrum of female power, spirituality, and energy and admonishes women to protect the sanctity of their vaginas from penis power, a compelling counterforce that can either bring life and vitality or diminish their vagina power and thereby threaten their spiritual equanimity.

In "Vagina Power," Alexyss exposes tricks of the "player trade" and urges women to seek justice for their vaginas rather than succumbing to "dickmatization," which means falling victim to the often predatory powers of the penis. She advises on male sexual anatomy and its potentially destructive influence on women, explaining that a man who is "living to ejaculate" is in a predator mode, causing women to fall prey to his seduction. Alexyss warns women not to succumb to the power of a well-seasoned sexually experienced male sex partner who knows how to hit the bottom and middle walls of their vaginas:

> And when the man is in a predator mode, he's gonna look for the weaknesses of a woman. A woman that's lonely. Her vagina is cold. She's layin' in bed at night playin' with her toys, or she's got a man beside her; he's a provider, but he's not hitting the walls and working the middle like that dog she's having the sneaky sex with.

Alexyss describes the penis as a powerful organ, a heat-seeking missile. She argues that "all penises are not created equal" and that some men have so much heat and intensity in their penis that you can feel it radiate through their clothes. "Just to touch the penis, it's on fire, it feels like it's fire underneath the skin," which causes many women to start going crazy:

> So if there's one hot like that, and he has the energy, and he knows how to work his hips, work his buttocks, and really twist her and bend her like she's a pretzel, give her the gratification she needs, she's going to be hooked and think that that's love or on a deeper root level. She's going to become sexually, mentally, and emotionally attached although he ain't no good.

Alexyss contends that once this sexually proficient man has his way, the woman is hooked on his penis power. She'll let him sneak in and out of her bedroom, while he continues to mistreat and neglect her, and "won't even buy you some shrimp from Long John Silvers, and that plate is what, $2.99?" But instead of taking you out to eat, Alexyss argues, "he can give you a mouthful of sperm and a rectum full of sperm." The woman will sacrifice and sell herself to keep him, "because the penis done ejaculated all up in her brain," and now the woman is in sexual bondage:

> He is screwing her into submission. He's screwing her into slavery by using the penis as a weapon to break her ass down! And her defenses! I mean she's wide open! With a penis all up in your vagina, man, you don't have no defenses!

Alexyss concludes "Vagina Power" by revealing that she teaches from her own experiences regarding how penis power can reduce a woman into a "cum freak."

Perhaps no other sexpert delineates the terror and awe of what male sexual proficiency can do for a woman quite like Alexyss Tylor; and no black woman in pop culture engages in a more frank discussion about the practicalities of sexual power. Accordingly, one of my students acknowledges that although she initially tunes into "Vagina Power" for educational purposes, watching the video inadvertently instigates her search for a male sexual partner "who knows how to work the middle and bottom vagina walls the way Alexyss describes." Hence, Alexyss' vivid appraisals of the power of good sex warn women not to fall into dickmatization, while her tantalizing discussions pique the imagination of women about sex's captivating capacity. Like Zane and Karrine Steffans, Alexyss Tylor offers women an entrancing revelation of how well executed sex can produce exhilaration.

Another YouTube video clip, "Two Faced Dick Wars," begins with her holding a brown plastic penis in each hand to illustrate that men have a righteous positive dick battling an evil negative dick on each shoulder:

> They have dick wars within their own mind. The top mind tries to be rational, tries to be fair, tries to be logical and keep all the agreements they've made. The other self, lower self, the evil dick, evil twin is all about what turns the dick on and what makes the nuts flair out and expand and tighten. Now it depends on which self your man is dominated by. Is he dominated by the high self, good dick head, or evil dick twin? Which brain is in control?

In "Dick Will Make You Slap Somebody," she tells the story of a woman who is having sex on top of a man and gets in such a groove and rhythm that the mere thought of another woman getting this same pleasure from him causes her to slap him right upside the head. In her "Halloween" video clip she is wary of men "rationing dick out to whomever they please." She discusses how unfaithful husbands see the wedding band as "a noose around the nuts, I mean a true nut bracket," and that many of them "take the wedding band off the finger and off the nuts and are running free to do whatever they want to do." Dressed in a black pilot's suit as her Halloween costume, she presses women to be pilots over their vaginas:

> I'm piloting the pussy; see y'all got to be a pilot over the pussy. Y'all got to be the pussy police because if y'all don't be careful these men that y'all are committing to; these boyfriends and these husbands are giving the dick away that's got to go up in your vagina. So the vagina is not safe because the men that are supposed to honor us, love us, respect us, and commit to us cannot be trusted.

In "Penis Power" she talks about the psychology of negative sperm power as a threat to a woman's equilibrium and how a woman's anatomy sets her up for the penis to sabotage her:

> A lot of women don't want to let the dick go. A lot of us are so caught up on one particular man's penis and the way he makes our vagina feel, and the way he makes our mouth feel, and the way he makes our total body feel when we're in bed with him and when he's inside of us and when he's talking with us, and when he's twisting us, and bending us all over in many kind of ways, asking us who's pussy it is and is it good to you?

She urges women to stop rationalizing the substandard behavior of their men and to stand in positive vagina power.

In "Black Pussy," Alexyss discusses her special interest in helping black women because "inside of the mind of the black woman's vagina is a state of emergency." She contends that many black women are susceptible to penis power because black mothers fail to educate their daughters on sexual matters. She asserts that mothers teach black girls to be nice and religious but at some point their daughters have to stop acting like little girls when they are dealing with "grown-ass men." In "Mama-Daughter Drama pt. 1," she addresses the abuse and devastating impact of older black women who dehumanize younger black women and how many black mothers and daughters have antagonistic relationships:

> There are a lot of black women that do not get along with their mothers and they love their mothers, they lie and die for their mothers, they go all out of their way trying to prove they're good enough and smart enough, they're wise enough, they're strong enough. They go out and get degrees because their mothers always told them, "You're gonna be a dumb stupid whore when you grow up."

Alexyss contends that such antagonism from mothers makes daughters susceptible to teenage pregnancy, abuse, and misfortune because they fail to provide daughters with love, acceptance, and sexual education. She urges black women to end this cycle because "these old-ass bitches need to be stopped!"

In "Hard Dicks and Tricks 2" she discusses how black women need to bring drive-by fucks to a standstill, and urges women to stop "liking the dick that don't like us." But not all of Alexyss Tylor's video clips bash men and their penis power. Some encourage women to delight in the pleasure of penis power and teach them how to proactively please their men sexually. In "Dick Talk," with plastic penis in hand, she instructs women: "We need to give dick what he needs, how he needs it, when he needs it," playfully adding, "even if dick needs to be choked a little bit, stroked a little bit, licked a little bit." She advises a woman to set aside time daily to talk to her man's dick, to have a dick conversation, and to learn the importance of dick massage. She caresses the head of her plastic penis, rubs it against her cheeks, and points out the intricate sensitive parts, "even up under the testicles, there are a lot of delicious places to go there, ladies." She invites women to learn how their men like them to touch and lick their penises and demonstrates how to stroke and go down the shaft of the penis. She argues that black couples are often sexually dysfunctional because they don't discuss words like "dick" and "pussy." Her video clip "Lollipop Lovin! Why Give Head" advises women to rethink their views on oral sex. She argues that though many women are told oral sex is nasty, defiles your body, or is against God, they should really see the penis as a beautiful piece of architecture created by God, "designed to be loved, smelled, tasted, touched, just truly honored and admired." She uses a lollipop to demonstrate proper ways of licking and sucking it, and even advises on types of lipstick that stay moist and work well on an actual penis. Some may accuse her of fetishizing the penis, but as Joanna Frueh points out, "Kissing a lover's penis is not necessarily anymore phallus-worshipping than kissing his back, foot, hair, or nipple" (1996: 15).

One of her most confrontational teachings is a two-part series entitled "Vagina Power in the Church." She presents the church as a sexual space and the pulpit as electrified with great spiritual-sexual energy, which makes it easy for women to get the emotions of their sexuality confused with the emotions of their spirituality while they worship God in church. She contends that the vibrations from music played in church connect with the spiritual-sexual aspects of the vagina and, similarly, the spiritual act of preaching does much to sexually stimulate both the preacher and his female congregants:

> Many preachers leave the pulpit with hard penises and highly elevated sex drives, ready and willing to tear a vagina up. This is perfectly normal and a very beautiful state to be in because he is at a pivotal point in the cosmic time realm because he has to make a responsible decision to ejaculate with purpose and intention that is designed to elevate the consciousness of the soul of a vagina.

Unfortunately, she argues, too many preachers choose a less enlightened path and sexually exploit women in their church. She grieves over the fact that people ignore how preachers degrade women in the black church, and that "women are raped and abused, degraded, humiliated, infected with sexually transmitted diseases in the black church" without fear of chastisement. She insists that women have aided and abetted such abusive patterns in the church for too long and that they must rise up, fight hypocrisy, and withhold contributions where necessary, particularly given that women are the backbone of the black church.

While Alexyss Tylor comes from the black church experience and her mother is an ordained minister, she rejects the label of "Christian" and instead brands herself as "spiritual woman." She is a vocal critic of the black church, claiming that much of the hurt and denial that pervades black sexual experiences has roots in black church teachings and hypocrisy. In a 2009 interview with KBOO Community Radio, Alexyss discusses how a lifetime of experience with black churches and Christians leads her to conclude, "Most people in church are dysfunctional regarding sex." In the same interview she condemns black preachers for creating a climate of spiritual and sexual hypocrisy by sweeping matters like homosexuality and clerical infidelity under the rug and for propagating ignorance and silence about sexual matters.

Alexyss alludes to the many hang-ups, issues, dysfunctions, and anxieties that she associates with the way black people approach sexuality, and her spiritual teachings attempt to re-socialize black people into seeing sex as something beautiful, powerful, and divine. She depicts the woman as a sacred temple of divine creation and often teaches how to use spiritual principles and meditative practices to achieve orgasm or begin the sexual healing process. Her video clip "Vagina Healing" shows women how to use a clear quartz crystal to bring positive energy, and how to anoint their bodies with olive oil to induce sacred healing. Alexyss walks through various steps with them including how to heal their breasts:

> Hold your breasts and apologize for letting anybody fuck our breasts that did not give a damn about us and that took nourishment and nutrients from our breasts and we know they were no fucking good. We demand that the energy that sustains our life return our breasts back to wholeness.

Alexyss continues this healing phase instructing women to tell their breasts, "I love you, honor you, respect you, and will never let anyone violate you again," while holding her breasts close to her, holding her nipples, and breathing the negative energy out. Such a ritual emanates from her insistence that spirituality is sexual and that sexuality is spiritual. Her teachings on sex charkas, the power of the body, the auric field, and her frequent allusions to the metaphysical realities of sperm presumably derive from her spiritual convictions, but also serve deliberate and strategic functions to re-condition the way black people view sex and spirituality.

We should credit Alexyss Tylor for creating an entirely new genre: the sensually comedic Internet morality play. Her sacred healing exercises and visual demonstrations with plastic penises and lollipops are deliberately excessive. Whether she is saluting the vagina, calling wedding rings "nut brackets," or talking about men screwing women into slavery, melodramatic absurdity is a big part of her dynamism and appeal. Several of my African-American female students make it a special event to gather together and watch her clips on YouTube. While they are laughing, they are also learning about the complexities of male and female relationships and ingesting her provocative sexual discourse and inimitable perspective on penis power. She captivates many black women because she talks in a fresh, graphic, and humorous way about lust, temptation, and sexual exploitation—topics often glossed over in discourses on sexual politics. Alexyss Tylor is an erotic revolutionary who inspires black women to stand up in vagina power and become proactive sexual subjects.

Gayle Rubin (1992) articulates how erotic preferences and erotic behavior demonstrate how patterns of subjective meanings and patterns of practice endure over space and time to organize social life. In this way, sexperts challenge enduring legacies of sexual inequality by debunking patriarchal myths that women are not sexually proactive, and empower women to tap into the wellspring of their sensuality. Their popular sex manuals suggest that black women are curious about sex and desire to be more-informed sex partners. Sexperts advise women on how to prepare and inform themselves for empowering sexual encounters. They provide proactive sexual scripts that help women protect themselves from broken hearts, exploitation, and sexually transmitted diseases. Sexperts alert women to the fact that they deserve to be sexually pleased and that they should be proactive participants in achieving such pleasure, even if it means employing a boy-toy or two, as LaDawn Black advises. They provide intriguing tips on how to indulge themselves with explosive sexual experiences.

Chapter Seven

Black Clergywomen and Sexual Discourse

The body is not meant for sexual immorality, but for the Lord

—Apostle Paul

Every day of my life I'm struggling to kill the flesh!

—Evangelist Juanita Bynum

This generation of women must begin to confess that we love God, and we love sex, too!

—Reverend Susan Newman

My good friend, whom I will call Alice, is a beautiful woman with a winsome personality and successful career. Her colleague Kevin is tall, athletic, witty, and confident—just how Alice likes her men. She tells me that they resonate physically and intellectually and form a magnetic attraction. So what's standing in the way of a steamy romance? Alice is serious about remaining celibate until she marries, and Kevin is resolute about having sex prior to deciding on marriage. So instead of viewing Kevin as a potential partner, Alice perceives him as a stumbling block to her faith.

Like many evangelical Christians, Alice wrestles with the daunting challenge of abstaining from sex while existing in a hyper-sexualized contemporary Western society. Whereas the poet Audre Lorde (1984) inspires women to give up self-negation and to see the erotic as an internal guiding power that can illuminate life, Alice interprets her sexual drives and passions as insubordinate factions warring against her spirituality. So Alice tries to suppress all erotic urges in order to maintain her spiritual ideals, which in this case means she must take great pains to avoid Kevin's path. While it is one thing for the Apostle Paul to instruct his contemporaries (who generally married before their late teens) to abstain from premarital sex, it is entirely a more arduous task to abide by such a mandate in today's world where a thirty-five-year-old black woman like Alice has few guarantees she will ever actually find a mate.

Katie Cannon (2004) argues that many black churchwomen, like Alice, grapple with two rival sexual realities: sex as a positive blessing when sanctioned by marriage for procreative purposes, or sex as a sinful indulgence that contaminates the spirit and mind. This Christian theme of negotiating spiritual idealism and sexual realism is a source of tension in the novels of James Baldwin, in particular *Go Tell It on the Mountain*, in which ministers denounce immorality and worldly pleasures to their congregants while secretly indulging in adulterous affairs and sinful activity. Baldwin portrays the black holiness church as a repository of sexual repression inevitably inciting such Christians to engage themselves in a precarious war against their own humanity. The church wields a cruel kind of psychic terrorism over Baldwin's protagonists, and instigates sexual struggles, which ultimately propel many to live double lives. Like Baldwin, several black female novelists explore how Christians navigate around the landmines of sexual temptation and desire in the black church.

Kimberla Lawson Roby uses Rev. Curtis Black as the protagonist of a three-novel series to expose dishonesty, greed, and sexual temptation within church leadership. In *Casting the First Stone*, Rev. Black becomes the pastor of a prestigious Chicago Baptist church. He gets lost in the allure of his newfound power, neglects his family, and kindles sexual affairs with women including the wife of a deacon. For much of the story his faithful wife Tanya considers leaving him, and finally takes charge over her life in a surprising ending. The humbled yet still deceptive Rev. Black appears in the sequel *Too Much of a Good Thing*, divorced and out of the pulpit. His greed and sexual indulgence continue after he remarries and pastors a new church. A near-death experience convinces him to clean up his ways as the Rev. appears in the third book *The Best-Kept Secret* as a devoted family man starting a new church and remaining faithful to Charlotte, his new younger wife of two years. Charlotte's wild sexcapades with his best friend Aaron anger Rev. Black enough to regress to his own sinful ways, but things ameliorate in the end. Roby's novels reflect the allure and intrigue as well as the betrayal and destruction that accompany sexual temptation in the black church.

Like Roby, other black female writers explore the conflict between spiritual values and sexual cravings. Ann Allen Shockley's novel *Say Jesus and Come to Me* depicts a female evangelist's attempt to balance the moral rigors of her preaching career alongside her lesbian relationship with a popular singer. After years of resisting, the evangelist comes to accept her sexual desire for

women, has fiery flings with women congregants in cities nationwide, and finally settles down with the vocalist before making their relationship public.

Michele Bowen's *Church Folk* includes femme fatales like Glodean who
provide pastors with sexual favors, while church leaders operate a prostitution ring out of a funeral home. ReShonda Tate Billingsley's *The Pastor's
Wife* has beautiful and flirtatious women trying to seduce their young pastor.
Victoria Murray's *Temptation* features three protagonists balancing Christian
values with their lusts and cravings. Additionally, Stephanie Perry-Moore
writes many novels that encourage teenage Christians to stay pure and holy
in the face of mounting pressure from their peers to have sex. These novels
reflect the dialectical tension between a society where media deluge people
with incessant flows of sex, and Christian ideals exhorting believers to wage
battle against their carnal desires. The preponderance of real-life sexual scandals in churches and among evangelical leaders demonstrates that such a fight
is easier said than won.

Marla Frederick contends that "significant to the experience of spirituality is the expression of sexuality" (2003: 186), and Traci West (2004) calls
for black churches to provide more discussion on this relationship. Ethicists
and sociologists point out that black churches often play a role in promoting
sexual reticence. Katie Cannon comments: "Black churchwomen are taught
that we must suppress the sexual aspect of our humanity, by reinforcing
norms and practices that proclaim procreational sex as a gift from God and
relational/recreational sex as the devil's handiwork" (2004: 12). Kelly Brown
Douglas and Emilie Townes implore black churches to break the cycle of
sexual repression by advancing an open and honest discourse on sexuality
(Douglas 1999). Juan Battle and Sandra Barnes depict the black church as
"a key harbinger of sexual conservatism and ill treatment of black sexual
minorities" (2009: 4). In the aforementioned documentary *Silence: In Search
of Black Female Sexuality in America*, Hilda Hutcherson argues that the
black church brands erotic pleasures like masturbation as sinful and Pastor
Jeremiah Wright argues that the black church is "tongue-tied" at the very
mention of sex. While many black clerics remain silent on contemporary issues of sexuality, three well-known clergywomen bring sexual discourse into
the fabric of black church life.

Don't let the provocative title of Ty Adams's popular book *Single, Saved,
and Having Sex* fool you; by her own account, the evangelist's days of getting busy under the sheets are far behind her. But it is her often-unsuccessful
attempts to live holy and curb her erotic desires that shed light on the plight
of many single Christian women grappling with celibacy. Her goal is to help
single women break free from what she calls the bondage of sexual sins. She
writes from the vantage point that "sex was created by God to be enjoyed

within the context of marriage of a man and a woman, period" (Adams 2006: 96), and that any sexual activity outside of marriage is sinful and detrimental to one's spiritual and emotional happiness.

Offering a theologically conservative perspective, Adams supplies liberals with much ammunition to dismiss *Single, Saved, and Having Sex* as sexually regressive. She proposes that sex outside of marriage leads to long-standing repercussions, which eventually can include separation from God and eternal judgment in hell. She contends that viewing pornography is immoral and she is even opposed to romantic kissing because "you only need one spark and it'll set your whole body on fire" (2006: 174). Adams urges readers to throw away condoms and birth control pills, asserting that they won't win the battle over their erotic drive while possessing a failure plan. She suggests that the only indemnity one needs is belief in God's power to help one refrain from sex prior to marriage.

Adams argues that masturbation generates confusion and heightens one's levels of discontent and emptiness. She not only maintains that masturbation is Satan's tool to tighten the grip of one's sexual lusts, but further alleges that fondling oneself opens the door to homosexual activity:

> If you are masturbating and you are a woman, then you are having sex with a woman and you invite a lesbian spirit upon you. If you are masturbating and you are a man, then you are having sex with a man and you invite a homosexual spirit upon you. You molest yourself, you are assaulting yourself and it will haunt you. (2006: 26)

Consistent with her theological conservatism, Adams presents homosexuality as sinful and unnatural, claiming that her past lesbian relationships were not the result of her natural attraction to women but rather the effect of a generational curse that plagues her family. In Adams's worldview, God does not allow a person to be born homosexual because "that would have automatically given you a destiny in hell" (2006: 64).

In light of such rather orthodox pronouncements, what, then, are the merits of including a hardcore evangelical like Ty Adams amongst a group of erotic revolutionaries? Her inclusion in such mix of luminaries derives from the fact that interwoven within her fundamentalist ideals and pious appeals to Christian purity resides an existential articulation of human lust and angst about controlling sexual urges that rarely engages sacred space. *Single, Saved, and Having Sex* certainly advises Christians to refrain from unmarried sex. Yet, in tackling the topic, Adams conjures up sexual fantasies and alludes to an inordinate amount of sex! Even the cover of her book has a sexy image of a man and woman in bed, presumably before or after a sexual encounter. Almost every page of her book includes some form of sexually explicit imagery, thus serving the inadvertent function of creating safe space for evangelical sexual discourse. The argument perhaps, is posited herein that explicit sexual discourse in the church, even from a restrictive evangelical vantage point, is better than no sexual discourse in the church at all. At the very least, the evangelist offers sexual scripts in sacred space that construct black female sexuality as powerful and alluring, hence requiring great restraint. This depiction of black female sexuality is certainly a helpful corrective to the politics of respectability that often constructs black female bodies as saintly and unsexy.

For an evangelical tome, the pages of the evangelist's book flood with conspicuous sexual content. She mentions how one of her friends abandons her husband and kids to become a lesbian striptease dancer. To underscore her points about sin, the evangelist offers countless statements with suggestive expressions like bumping and grinding, putting your mouth on sexual organs, knowing where your "spot" is, and becoming imprisoned by the grip of masturbation. She offers an unprecedented interpretation of a popular Bible passage (Judges 16:19), in which she claims that Delilah performs oral sex on Samson to lull him to sleep and shave off his hair. She gives a shocking account of how one of her relatives performs sexual acts with a man for money and allows him access to her eleven-year-old daughter to fulfill his fantasy of having sex with a virgin.

Adams' transparency about her own sexual history and transgressions is equally staggering in light of the resounding silence of many of her black evangelical peers regarding sexual matters:

> I was the woman with many boyfriends-made-husbands. I was thirsty, and none of my lovers quenched my thirst. I used sexual relationships to cover up the emptiness inside of me that had built up from childhood. I was damaged as a child by the hands of men who violated and sexually molested me. I was heavily exposed to homosexuality, incestuous relationships, and sexual perversion. (2006: 51-52)

She recalls how she spends years partaking in a world of homosexuality, a rare admission for an evangelical spiritual leader. After she becomes a Christian, she does not immediately give up her promiscuous lifestyle, going to church on Sunday morning and rolling back under the sheets in wild sexual passion later that night. She talks about the shame, pain, and confusion she experiences from staging her new spiritual ideals against her strong erotic drives. Finally deciding to make a clean break from a sinful past, "I picked up the phone and called this woman whom I was living in sin with and said, 'I'm not coming back. . . . I can't choose you over Jesus'" (2006: 58). Notwithstanding her newfound resolve, she reveals that periods of chastity are followed by more sexual binges.

With the pervasive force of homophobia wielding its power on sexual politics in black churches, a prominent spiritual leader candidly reflecting on a past life in homosexual activity is an extraordinarily rare occurrence. While her condemnation of homosexual activity supports heterosexist hegemony and is no doubt regressive, the mere utterance of her enduring struggle with same-sex erotic urges and sexual practices validates the erotic experiences of presumably numerous other evangelicals dealing with similar same-sex longings and relationships, and hence has overtly political ramifications if not intent. Black churches often pay no attention to the issue of homosexuality (Douglass 1999), and when leaders do broach the topic, it is rarely done in the pervasive manner of Adams who constructs the same-sex lifestyle as so alluring an alternative as to necessitate resistance. Adams's forthright discussion confirms that black female bodies can receive sexual pleasure outside of the contours of heteronormativity, a reality that spiritual leaders rarely mention. By admitting that her exit from the same-sex lifestyle was a long hard slog, Adams unwittingly discloses that same-sex activity can compete in the "erotic marketplace," and such a tacit acknowledgement may pique the interest of curious onlookers to explore why leaving that world entails such a difficult battle. In this way, Adams' candid remarks about her same-sex sexual binges and erotic entrapments unintentionally exert subversive sexual scripts to sacred space.

Adams contributes to sexual discourse by tempering her spiritual ideals with sexual realism. She estimates that seventy percent of all unmarried Christians are "saved and having sex," and even concedes that too many ministers are sleeping with their members. She discusses how sexual urges are natural components of our humanity and how she receives thousands of emails from sexually damaged Christians disclosing their struggles to keep their sexual desires in check. She admits that there is no pill in a bottle or universal panacea to totally revoke one's lusts, and informs that cold showers don't work. From Adams' candid admissions we learn that her struggle to keep her erotic fountainhead in check proves an arduous task, giving credence to the Apostle Paul's caveat that sexual chastity requires a spiritual gift (1 Corinthians 7:7) and Jesus' admonition that "the spirit is willing but the flesh is weak" (Matthew 26:41).

The assurance that *Single, Saved, and Having Sex* is a book about black Christian women and their sexual longings single-handedly makes it an important contribution to black sexual discourse, if not for any other reason than the fact that black female clergy invading sacred space with sexual discourse is in itself a political act against male domination. Ty Adams' revelations of her sexual struggles serve a manifest function to promote chastity, yet also a latent function to illustrate the extreme difficulty, if not absurdity, of a sexually charged Christian woman remaining celibate until marriage. Although she offers no resolutions concerning one's battle to subdue one's lust, her mere establishment of a sexual discourse in which Christian women can discuss their passions and drives is an incidental feminist achievement, particularly in the evangelical context in which it resides.

Like Adams, another popular evangelist named Juanita Bynum writes and preaches about her past and present sexual struggles to keep her flesh in check. In a September 2007 cover story, *The New York Times* describes Juanita Bynum as the most prominent black female television evangelist in the country. The article's purpose is not to celebrate Bynum's preeminence but rather to report on her bout of domestic violence in which her then-husband, Bishop Thomas Weeks, is alleged to have physically assaulted her in a hotel parking lot. The allegation draws immense media attention as newspapers and television stations cover her troubled marriage, pending divorce, and new ministry focus on domestic violence. But Juanita Bynum is already one of the most recognizable preachers in the black church prior to such headlines. She emerges on the national scene years earlier than what will be her second marriage to Bishop Weeks, as an initially divorced preacher addressing the existential needs of her contemporaries. Flying under the evangelical radar for most of the 1990s, Bynum becomes a household name in 1998 when T.D. Jakes, a popular mega-church pastor and businessman, invites her to keynote his women's conference in Atlanta. Seizing the moment, the evangelist preaches a provocative sermon called "No More Sheets." The video of the sermon sells over a million copies, demonstrating its cultural significance among black women and reminding us that sex sells, even in Christendom.

"No More Sheets" offers tantalizing details about Bynum's struggles on welfare, sexual longings and transgressions, destructive romantic relationships, painful first divorce, and attempted suicide, all shrouded with a renewed faith and dependence upon God. The sermon also sparks "No More Sheets" parties nationwide in which black women assemble in alternating homes to watch the video and encourage each other toward sexual purity. Ten years later, it still remains the preeminent sermon addressing the struggles of many black Christian women to remain celibate and holy before God while negotiating the passions and sexual longings requisite in their humanity.

Bynum begins "No More Sheets" by revealing how she feels vulnerable and naked in fulfilling God's mandate to address issues she and others face as single women. You can see the angst and fright on her face as she tells her audience, "I'm scared about this message." She discusses her failed first marriage and divorce and the trauma of being single again and remaining holy because everywhere she goes she sees a fine man and she keeps wondering to herself, "When is it going to be my turn? What am I doing wrong?"

Bynum is transparent about past transgressions throughout most of the message. She talks about a not-so-distant period of her life when she sleeps with many men and depends on them for sex, clothes, and money. She gives intimate details about her ex-boyfriends, three miscarriages, and the nervous breakdown that lead to her institutionalization. She laments not being married and rejects trite consolations from married women uninitiated with her struggle:

> I find it very difficult to listen to anybody preach to me about being single when they got a pair of thighs in their bed every night, you know, with you rolling over in the sheets, and you telling me to "hold on honey, sanctify yourself," and you're going home to biceps and triceps, big old muscles and thighs and you got somebody giving you back rubs. No! No! No! You go and sit down. I want to hear "hold on" from somebody who is really holding on!

Bynum engages frank discussions on taboo topics like masturbation and sexual addiction, discloses her current battles with sexual temptations, and addresses contemporary problems many men and women face that clergy often overlook. She conveys how God took her through a process of prayer and fasting to purge her from the spiritual and emotional baggage she carried from previous sexual partners. At one point in the sermon, she wraps sheets around her and removes them one by one to demonstrate God's delivering power from the layers of bondage that plague her from past sexual relationships. This is unusually candid sexual discourse for a sermon.

After enjoying national acclaim for "No More Sheets," Bynum remarries in 2003 and continues making sex an important part of her message. In her popular sermon "Pride vs. the Proverbs 31 Woman" she tells her audience: "We're going to talk about some real sex. Some of y'all ain't doing it right. Somebody got to help you!" She urges women to learn how to minister to their husbands sexually and orders them to "Put that Bible down and put a negligee on and work it!" Throughout the sermon she brags about her sexual prowess with innuendos like, "That's why [then-husband Bishop Weeks] comes in preaching and happy!" She says when a man comes home from work he does not want to hear her praying in tongues, he wants some sex and lots of it. She argues that Christian wives need to stop being sexually timid and warns, "If you close your legs somebody else is going to open her legs to your husband." In another sermon "Sex, But No Romance," Bynum tells women, "You've got to know what the man in the church needs; men need sex, ladies." In the same sermon she calls herself the Dr. Ruth of Christendom.

Like Ty Adams, Juanita Bynum teaches from the vantage point of an evangelical perspective concerning biblical prescriptions on sex and sin. Both evangelists offer no practical solution for women to control combustible lusts and sexual cravings beyond more prayer, more Bible reading, and more fasting. In this regard, many feminists will scrutinize Adams and Bynum for encouraging women to hold off on sex and masturbation until they are married. Such a mandate relegates many black women to a lifetime of celibacy when considering today's depleted pool of eligible black Christian male prospects for marriage. Similarly, other feminists would justifiably find fault with Bynum for putting the onus on women to coddle their husbands' sexual fantasies, as well as the overall conservative tone that characterizes Adams' denigration of homosexuality and prescriptions for spiritual purity.

Notwithstanding the regressive elements of their sexual politics, Adams' and Bynum's books and sermons provide honest discourses on sexual realism. Bynum is one of the first black preachers to talk about masturbation behind the pulpit on a national stage; Adams' book has no equal among evangelicals as a candid reflection of one's sexual resume. These evangelists disrupt traditional sexual scripts of feminine sexual passivity and present the black female body as a repository of intense sexual desire. They inspire many Christian women to be transparent about their longings and passions and to see themselves as sexual beings. Taken in context, this may amount to an important step in disabusing what Kelly Brown Douglas (1999) perceives as a sexually repressed and sexually reticent black church culture.

Susan Newman is another nationally recognized preacher and writer whose message and ministry will unquestionably resonate more with sex-positive feminists than the efforts of Adams and Bynum. Newman becomes a Christian at age thirteen, an ordained minister in her twenties, and serves as pastor or associate pastor in several churches for much of her adult life. She offers sermons, keynote speeches, church workshops, and an entire book on the topic of sex, while raising the consciousness of black churches nationwide concerning HIV/AIDS testing and awareness. Yet Newman approaches sex from a different vantage point than Ty Adams and Juanita Bynum. In her book *OH GOD!: A Black Woman's Guide to Sex and Spirituality*, Newman adopts a more theologically liberal approach to balancing Christian ideals with sexual realism.

Newman draws from her exegetical training to revisit biblical mandates against premarital sex. Since the Apostle Paul is the only biblical writer who prohibits sex outside of marriage, Newman takes the task of dismantling the credibility of his mandates. She points out that Paul succeeds in "stamping Christianity with a loathing of sex and the body from which we have never fully recovered" (2002: 14). Instead of interpreting Paul's teachings literally and as the inspired word of God, she conceptualizes his mandates within the scope of the apostle's own values and prejudices. She reminds us that Paul's entire letter to Philemon condones slavery and that he also confers sexist instructions for the Corinthians to silence their women in church (1 Corinthians 14:33-35) largely because he is functioning in an era where slavery is rampant and women are viewed as inferior. Playfully alluding to Paul's endorsement of slavery and sexism, Newman aptly concludes, "So, if you are going to be a literalist when it comes to Paul's instructions, then, black women, forget about an orgasm, and just shut your mouths and go back to ole massa's plantation and pick a bale of cotton" (2002: 16)!

Newman draws distinctions between the way people perceive women in first-century Palestine and in today's American culture, to argue that "the women in the Bible simply are not us!" (2002: 32), in that they couldn't own property and were almost totally at the disposal of men. She adds:

> Women in ancient civilizations did not have to deal with sexual abstinence as women do today; girls were betrothed at the age of five and given in marriage between the ages of thirteen and sixteen. However, today we have women who go to college, pursue careers, and sometimes delay marriage and childbearing. There are some women who choose not to marry and have children. (2002: 35)

Newman postulates that every statement in Paul's letters is not prescriptive for all ages and all people because women in biblical times had to plot their course in an oppressive and unjust patriarchal society. She reminds Christians that it was Paul, not Jesus, who precludes sex outside of marriage and that Jesus, while silent on this issue, did everything to press forward the status of women and renovate their prospects for a full life. Whereas conservative evangelicals perceive all of Paul's writings as probative, theological liberals can contextually view some as instructive, while rejecting others, hence opening the door for counter-narratives to biblical mandates. We see that Newman takes the more liberal route in situating Paul's mandates against pre-marital sex within the context of Hellenistic patriarchy.

After discrediting the very biblical prognosticator who keeps many Christian women beleaguered to control their sexual appetites, Susan Newman projects an agenda for women to reclaim their bodies from Paul's grasp. She attacks the more conservative black church's anti-dance stance, arguing that dancing is a celebration of life for black people and functions as a healthy practice field to negotiate sexual emotions and feelings in young people. She also challenges the double standard of women holding out on enjoying sex until they marry, while men in the church freely indulge in sexual intimacies. Newman pushes for women to take over their bodies by telling their lovers what sexually pleases them and to decline judging their bodies by mass media images of female physical perfection. She also invites women to reject church dictums that prohibit contraceptive use, insisting that the Catholic Church is not the arbiter of legislation regarding what women can and cannot do with their bodies.

Newman inspires women to see their sex drive as a natural and healthy component of who they are as God's creation. She perceives an invisible barrier that obstructs many women from embracing their sexual selves; usually this barrier comes in the form of shame and abuse that prevent women from enjoying a healthy sex life. She alludes to a silent sisterhood of thousands of women who exhibit what she calls "sexual schizophrenia" by living in guilt and shame for lack of a way to merge their spiritual and sexual selves:

> It's like living two lives. The one persona goes to church, is a member of the singles ministry, sings in the gospel choir, belongs to the Women's Fellowship, and mentors young girls in the community. The other persona goes to church, is sexually frustrated, is a member of the singles ministry, and feels guilty when she masturbates, sings in the gospel choir, is desperately trying to find a husband, belongs to the Women's Fellowship, and mentors young girls in the community. Same person, but a divided, tortured existence, searching for healthy, spiritually acceptable ways to satisfy sexual yearnings. (2002: 93)

She argues that sexual schizophrenia occurs in women who try to be spiritual and yet systematically repress any form of sexuality in their lives. Newman reiterates that it is harmful for the church to encourage women to forgo erotic expression until they are married, and instead offers unmarried women practical advice on how to choose sexual partners carefully. Like Zane, she warns against the potential dangers of sexual intimacy, comparing multiple sex partners to playing Russian Roulette: "You never know which shot will be the lethal one" (2002: 119). Newman takes the reader through several hypothetical situations to explore pitfalls and misunderstandings in sexual relationships, and empowers each individual to make proactive decisions toward crafting her own healthy sexual life in this age of HIV/AIDS. Newman advocates for Christians to always carry a condom, unlike Ty Adams who perceives this as a failure plan.

While Adams and Bynum render masturbation as sinful and potentially destructive, Newman portrays self-pleasuring to be as normal as the air we breathe, in itself incapable of producing emotional, physical, or spiritual harm. She blasts away at preachers who teach that masturbation is an evil demonic tool because of their misinterpretation of a biblical passage (Genesis 38:6-26) in which God punishes Onan for "spilling his seed." She argues that the sin of Onan is not masturbation, as some preachers proclaim, but is his refusal to comply with the Levite Law and procreate with his dead brother's wife. She advocates for Christians to perceive self-pleasuring as a normal and healthy part of their sexuality:

> Some religious leaders believe and teach that self-pleasuring is wrong; however, I hope that, as you are reassessing your beliefs and attitudes, you will open your

spirit and mind to the natural act of pleasuring yourself. How can you share with your lover what will arouse and please you if you do not know firsthand for yourself? (2002: 132)

She adds that God created our bodies to be instruments of sensual pleasure and that self-touch helps us fully ascertain our sexual selves.

Newman presents sexual decisions—having a loving partner, whether or not to masturbate, when to initiate sex, etc.—as choices that exist within the woman's body and therefore are hers and hers alone to make. She believes celibacy can be a healthy act when women approach it as a wonderful sexual preference, rather than a mandate for single Christians. Celibacy, she argues, is a choice to be made in joy and peace, not a decision tinged with frustration and anger, which is often the case among Christians who reluctantly resist erotic urges while heeding spiritual proscriptions against all forms of sexual activity. Newman compares the black church to a dysfunctional family when it comes to sexual issues, and claims that it spends far too much time arguing whether or not HIV/AIDS is God's judgment against homosexuality, rather than empowering members to be responsible sexual agents. She argues that since women make up a larger contingency of the black church, black women suffer disproportionately from the brunt of its regressive sexual politics.

From the perspective of scripting theory, Newman rejects discursive practices that deploy sexuality as a strategy to contain women's bodies. She ends the book campaigning for the black church and black women to embrace a new sexual ethic that promotes the individual's freedom to choose how she expresses herself sexually. She calls for an open and honest dialogue on sex, and for women to plan carefully every aspect of their lives including their sexual relationships. She normalizes women having healthy libidos and heartens them to keep sex as an important aspect of their lives. Commensurate with poet Audre Lorde's call for women to embrace their inward erotic guide, Rev. Susan Newman reminds women that "to be sexually aroused and then try to deny our body's natural expression is to deny the very essence of who God created us to be—sexual beings, with spirit, mind, heart, and soul" (2002: 165).

Susan Newman uses hermeneutical tools, historical arguments, and good ole fashioned folk wisdom in an attempt to dissuade women from perceiving their erotic desires and spiritual ideals as warring factions. Because the vast majority of black churches are theologically conservative, many black women will perceive Newman's grumbling against the Apostle Paul as blasphemous, and will instead opt to embrace the theologically conservative (but no less sexually provocative) ruminations of Ty Adams and Juanita

Bynum. While finding themselves on different sides of the spectrum, these three spiritual women create new and intriguing spaces in Christendom for sexual discourse, challenging the politics of silence by hook or by crook. These erotic revolutionaries introduce sacred space to discursive strategies that depict the vibrancy of female sexuality and help women negotiate erotic desires with spiritual ideals.

Chapter Eight

Erotic Queens of Comedy

You know Moms' been accused of liking young men and I'm guilty. Can't no old man do nothing for me except bring me a message from a younger man.

—Jackie "Moms" Mabley

Every woman doesn't want to be in love with you. Some of us just want to fuck. We don't want to know your name; we don't want to hear about your problems. Matter of fact; don't pull your pants down too far cause you're not staying very long. Hurry up and eat this pussy before my kids wake up.

—Sheryl Underwood

A group of friends take me out to a comedy event in New Orleans to celebrate my birthday. All the comics are great but Melanie, the lone comedienne of the event, steals the show. From the moment she steps on the stage, Melanie discharges a verbal blitzkrieg on men and their sexual inadequacies. She talks about everything from small penises and erectile dysfunction to "dirty draws" and "smelly balls," triggering raucous laughter from the women, which slightly upstages the vexing scowls on the faces of the men. In a world where men reign over comedic content, Melanie flips the script by putting men up for rigorous scrutiny as objects of ridicule, defenseless pawns for mockery before hundreds of female audience members. Melanie's routine reveals the power of the black female comic performer as "heckler" of the status quo.

"Within the topsy-turvy world of stand-up comp performance, hierarchies are inverted, power relations are subverted and a good time is had by all" (Gilbert 2004: xii). Bambi Haggins (2007) reveals how black female comics deconstruct gendered expectations and subversively expand the boundaries of black female performance. They wield rhetorical power by engaging in a public, socially authorized, conversation about their experiences and enjoy great latitude to engage taboo topics like sex and sexuality, transforming comedy into a distinctive arena of sexual discourse. They shove propriety aside and unflinchingly sexualize men with the most artfully embarrassing uses of wit. Black female comics also make the most of opportunities to challenge repressive sexual politics pertaining to women. They broadcast the frustrations of many of the voiceless black women in the audience and censure men for their lack of sexual creativity, infidelity, and other sexual transgressions against women. They present their bodies as sexual bodies, and are unashamed to revel in the lusts of the flesh.

Jackie "Moms" Mabley is one of the earliest black female comics to engage in public sexual discourse. A weekly fixture at Harlem's Apollo Theatre in the 1950s, her visibility expands as she appears on television and in movies and plays Carnegie Hall in the 1960s. The writer and poet Jewelle Gomez describes Mabley's edgy shtick and disarming persona:

> She remained a dowdy mess with a profane (and toothless) mouth. Wearing oversized shoes, a frumpy dress, and a cap, she looked like someone's rural aunt up for a visit. But the gist of her routines was to outline her personal sexual appetite, her coda being: there was nothing an old man could do for her except show her the way to a young man. (Gomez 1993: 31-32)

Contemporary black comediennes who broadcast their lust for younger men are beholden to Mabley. Her penchant for alluding to female sexual needs and cleverly underscoring the inability of men to satisfy such needs was off-limits for comediennes until recently (Williams 1995). Mabley's routines were replete with short stories that portrayed female protagonists as aggressive sexual agents, lusting after men, cheating on their husbands, and getting caught running around town with other men. Though remarkably foreshadowing, the sexual innuendos and interplay in Moms Mabley's sets are nevertheless mild in comparison to the content of contemporary black female comics.

Like Mabley, comic legend Whoopi Goldberg provides frank discussions on female sexuality. In her autobiography entitled *Book*, Whoopi offers a liberal perspective on political sex scandals arguing, "just because a guy gets his tip wet once in a while, it doesn't make him a bad president. It doesn't even make him a bad guy" (Goldberg 1999:19). She also believes masturbation should be taught to kids in school, and regrets the fact that the United States carries a lot of "fucked-up Puritan baggage about sex in general" (1999: 135). She exhorts women to dump men who refuse to reciprocate oral pleasure, and scolds men for not wiping off their penises correctly after urinating: "Men live by the shake, but wiping makes so much more sense" (1999: 227). Outside of the comedy realm, women have few public opportunities to address the absurdities of phallic maintenance.

In her 2007 show *The Word According to Whoopi*, the comic jokes about how the birth control pill took women's fear of sex away, and brags, "I can now have sex with anybody I want." She discusses earlier days when she would go to Central Park without underwear to score some quick action (she gyrates on the stage to simulate her sexing a stranger she just met in the park). She grumbles about how aging means her sexual juices don't start up so quickly and that just staying awake during sex is now a great challenge. She finishes her set by claiming how today's younger black females leave her in the dust when it comes to graphic references to sex and sexuality on stage. Perhaps Whoopi is alluding to someone like Wanda Sykes, who is rarely short on sexual discourse.

In her 2007 performance in Seattle *Wanda Sykes: Sick and Tired*, the actress and comedienne admits that during road trips she watches a lot of porn in hotels and masturbates while hyping herself up: "You work that shit don't you bitch, come on, fuck it like that, yes, I'm good, I'm good!" She also offers an interesting commentary on men and dogs:

> I hate when women compare men to dogs; we've got to stop doing that ladies, you know, "men are dogs." We've got to stop that, men are not dogs; dogs are loyal. Come on guys, I've never found any strange panties in my dog's house. Dogs are great, they never leave you, they're there for you and they can lick their own balls.

Wanda's set touches on everything from abortion rights and women's sexual freedom, to the art of detecting artificial breasts: "You know, if titties are identical they're fake." More recently, in her 2009 performance at the Warner Theatre in Washington D.C. entitled *Wanda Sykes: I'ma Be Me*, the comic offers more sexual discourse including a risqué commentary on President Obama and his wife's sex life, arguing, "There's some good hot sex goin' on at 1600 Pennsylvania Avenue; I mean we talking ass-slappin' hair pullin'" [she gyrates to simulate the president penetrating his wife from behind]. She suggests they should put a sign out on the White House lawn saying, "If the White House is rocking, don't come knocking." Wanda represents a trend among black female comics to sexualize sitting presidents, a seditious move that offers graphic images of the most powerful men in the world engaging in private acts of eroticism. In this way female comics flex their muscles by warning men in high places that they are not immune to the deluge of sexual ridicule.

But Wanda's show in Washington D.C. is significant for more reasons than taking jabs at President Obama. She made history as the first noted

African-American comic to integrate stories about her same-sex spouse into a set. Her first casual reference to "my wife" in one of her anecdotes is one small statement for Wanda and one discursive leap for black sexual politics. Later in the set she gets more aggressive with her personal life, revealing that her previous decision to "come out" was inextricably linked to her outrage regarding Proposition 8, a California ballot initiative passed in 2008 that officially declared same-sex marriage invalid in the state. She then alleges that it is more difficult being gay than black because "I didn't have to come out black! I didn't have to sit my parents down and tell them about my blackness!" Scoffing at the suggestion that homosexuality is a choice, she comments, "I'm sure a lot of straight guys in here on several occasions probably think: 'You know, I think I'ma suck a dick today. Nah, I choose not to.'" Her denunciations of heterosexism aside, she does not exclude gay men from ridicule in her set. Vacationing on a gay cruise with 3200 men, she warns her wife that "getting in that pool is like swimming in a bowl of thick soup. . . . You get in that pool, nine months later we sittin' on Maury Povich trying to find the baby daddy." Her jabs at gays demonstrate that for Wanda, all men—from President Obama to "broke dick Bob," the star of penis enhancement commercials—are fair game for sexual mockery.

Wanda also chats about the vicissitudes of being the mother of white twins, including her fear that if they ever got separated from her at Disneyland, she'd have to hire a white woman to reclaim them. She frames life with her French spouse and white kids as having its own unique challenges but also as normal, healthy, and happy, a discursive slam-dunk on heteronormativity. She discusses her wife and children from a vantage point of strength, taking it for granted that her family life is fair game in her set even if it is no doubt offensive to some members of her audiences. Wanda's transparency about her same-sex marriage is a revolutionary move that demonstrates the black female comic's penchant for subverting dominant narratives of sexuality. As Whoopi and Wanda consign themselves to elder stateswomen roles in the comic realm, a younger breed of black comediennes has taken even more liberties in lacing sets with explicit sexual content that challenges the politics of respectability.

BET's nightly television program *Comic View* showcases up-and-coming black comics in front of a national television audience. Although male comics generally outnumber females four to one, the show offers the rare platform for black women to engage in black sexual politics before millions of viewers. For example, during Sherri Sinclair's *Comic View* performance, she brags about liking young thugs and tells a guy in the audience that he's too old for her because "I bet your penis got asthma," imitating his erect penis having an asthma attack and going soft. She turns to another male victim to inquire about his age and then respond, "Twenty-five? Ooooh, see I would pluck the hell out of you!" Note that, in contrast to patriarchal sexual scripts that reject the aging female body and valorize younger women, Sherri gives men a taste of their own medicine by ridiculing older male bodies and expressing overt lust after a younger man. Moments later Sherri comments on oral sex:

> Men like to be hooked up too, they like the oral sex. How many of you ladies are hooking your man up? Some of you fellows want to be hooked up, I understand. But some of you fellows need to clean up! Some of y'all got them salty nuts, and I got high blood pressure!

She regrets recently licking her man in the no-fly zone because every time she comes home from work, "he got his legs up behind his ears" waiting for an encore.

Sylvia's appearance on *Comic View* includes comments concerning her boyfriend's inability to please her orally. One night during sex she asks him to "go downtown" and he mistakenly gets up, puts on his clothes, and starts the car. She talks about another sexual encounter with her "biscuit-eating" country boyfriend: "One night I'm working him, I'm working him, I'm working him. All of a sudden he said, 'oh baby damn that's good.' I reached over and flip on the light switch and this fool is eating a cupcake!" Another boyfriend requests her to go downtown on him in honor of Black History Month, and she recalls, "I went down and turned into a true slave y'all." Later she jokes about Oprah being gay and having enough money to buy any woman in the arena, adding that she'd tell Oprah, "Girlfriend, I ain't eating no coochie, but I will vibrate your big butt to death." In the span of a few minutes, Sylvia goes from ridiculing an ignorant sex partner and greedy boyfriend, to making fun of her own compliance to another boyfriend's absurd appeal for fellatio, to negotiating same-sex eroticism with Oprah.

When Dawn B appears on *Comic View*, she discusses her first sexual experience with a well-endowed thug. Upon viewing his private part she responds, "Damn! Is that all you? Get me a camera, I need to take a picture of this!" To prepare for his length, she demonstrates how she warms up with her "big dick" stretching exercise. Dawn later mulls over how holding her urine for ten minutes longer is orgasmic. Retha Jones appears on *Comic View* complaining about men who brag about their sexual prowess yet when it's time to show and prove, they merely perform for two minutes, turn over, start snoring and breaking wind. Annie McKnight hits the stage grumbling about the effect Viagra is having on sugar daddies: "Back in the day, the old sugar daddy just wanted to smell your panties, now thanks to Viagra, they want to wear your ass out." BET often rebroadcasts *Comic View* performances, giving black comediennes even more opportunities to capture millions of viewers with their unique brand of sexual politics. It is one of the rare opportunities where black women can lust after younger men, ridicule penis size or function, allude to oral sex, and present themselves as proactive sexual agents before a mass audience.

HBO's *Def Comedy Jam* is another television show that showcases black comics and launches the careers of highly acclaimed comediennes like Adele Givens, Barbara Carlisle, and Sheryl Underwood. HBO allocates graphic adult content, which bodes well for highly erotic sets. Performances on *Def Comedy Jam* set new standards for how black women address sexual topics by featuring several black comediennes and their unique brands of raunchy humor and risqué sexual politics. (You can view the *Def Comedy Jam* performances discussed bellow on *Russell Simmons' Def Comedy Jam All Stars DVD series*)

Barbara Carlisle begins her *Def Comedy Jam* appearance by getting some proverbial "fuck you's" out of the way, pointing to one member in the audience, "fuck you," and to another, "fuck you," repeating this practice until she points to the last guy standing and tells him "and you, ooooooh, fuck me please." Moments later Barbara offers her revised rendition of a popular bedtime story:

> Little Red Riding Hood was walking through the woods one day. The big bad wolf jumped out of the bushes and said, "Little Red Riding Hood, I'm gonna throw you down and fuck you to death." Little Red Riding Hood said, "No you ain't! You gonna eat me just like the book says."

With such an absurd play on words, Barbara demonstrates that even the pristine Little Red Riding Hood is fair game to be sexualized. She continues with more sexual absurdity, discussing how she used to "suck dick" long before it became fashionable but had to quit because of medical complications when her boyfriend neglected to tell her that he ate seafood, to which she is allergic, necessitating her being rushed to the Emergency room. Her moratorium on oral sex proves short-lived because "old habits are hard to break." She then recalls another absurd accident:

> This time I had done a little reading up on it. In the book it say well ya got to be really freaky with it. So I went to reach down there and lick his balls. His Goddamn dick stuck me dead in the eye. They rush me to the hospital; doctor said a few more inches it would have put my eye out.

Barbara then reveals that instead of counting sheep to go to sleep, she counts penises. Taking a few pokes at men, she talks about how this guy she was dating asked her why she never tells him when she's having an orgasm, her response being "you're never around when it happens." She mentions a book she is writing called *Short Dick Men: Are They Taking Over?* She ends her set recalling an instance when her boyfriend proclaimed, "Barbara, you know there's an art to love making," to which she replied, "Oh yeah? Well I wish somebody would draw you a bigger dick!" With these absurd sex stories and personal revelations, Barbara inadvertently de-stigmatizes oral sex and sanctions female lust, expresses disdain for poor sexual performances, and mocks male sexual anatomy, a discursive blow to the politics of respectability.

Yvette Wilson's *Def Comedy Jam* set begins with her complimenting a man in the audience for being so cute. While he proudly stands up to show himself to the crowd, Yvette continues, "Look at him, he's just as cute and grinning. You know when they grin like that they can't fuck," which catches her victim and audience off guard. Two minutes later, Yvette gyrates to imitate her ex-boyfriend fucking off beat before sharing why she only messes with ugly men: because they always "bring it" in the bedroom to compensate for their looks. Hence Yvette not only mocks men as sex partners, but also condones using ugly men as sexual "tools," borrowing a page from men who joke about putting bags over the faces of unattractive woman during intercourse.

On the same night Yvette performs, a comic named "Mugga" talks about how everything is going well with a Muslim guy she's dating "until the brotha came home and told me he don't eat no pussy, because it's pork." She boastfully adds: "I got rid of his ass and got me a good pussy-eating Christian—Let the church say Amen!" This joke works so well because of the ironic mixing of religious identity with preferences and practices in oral sex. It also demonstrates a woman insisting that a man pleasure her orally, instead of fretting how to conform to her man's sexual whims and fantasies, as popular sexual discourse often dictates. The stage at *Def Comedy Jam*, as well as local venues in cities nationwide, is safe space for black women to control sexual discourse, celebrate their voracious sexual appetites, and air dirty laundry about the men in their lives, as well as mocking their own sexual representation. No doubt, for many audience members black female comic sets represent their first exposure to women publicly controlling sexual discourse.

Although men still dominate the world of comedy, an increasing number of black women are carving out unique space to display their wit and in-your-face commentary. As part of their national tour, Adele Givens, Miss Laura Hayes, Sommore, and Mo'Nique make a movie of their performance in the Memphis Orpheum Theatre called *The Queens of Comedy* (2001). The movie is reminiscent of Spike Lee's production *The Kings of Comedy* released several years earlier and is the first movie to showcase the talents of multiple female comics performing at one event. *The Queens of Comedy's* popular reception demonstrates the increasing role black comediennes wield in popular culture.

Miss Laura keeps things rolling as the MC of the night, introducing her own brand of humor in between sets including a sketch where she puts a microphone in her groin area to simulate a man's erect penis. Adele Givens' performance in *The Queens of Comedy* movie is quite subdued compared to her set in the *Platinum Comedy Series* (a DVD series of special performances featuring the leading black comics) in 2004. In the *Platinum Comedy Series* she tells religious women, "God said be holy; He didn't say you can't be sexy," and refers to her two sons as cock-blockers: "You can't even fuck in your house like you used to. Girl I used to go in my kitchen and get a dick sandwich anytime I felt like it. These little bastards got me on a diet and I don't appreciate it!" She discusses how she has to be careful trying to get some from her man because the last thing she wants is for her sons "to catch Mama's ass tossed up like a Caesar salad." Adele then chides vocalist and music producer R. Kelly for making a sex videotape with a minor, but admits "I would fuck Usher and go to jail happy." She also brags about masturbating all the time and ends her set with a song she wrote ridiculing men who date hos and don't know it.

While Adele's performance in *The Queens of Comedy* is somewhat tame, Sommore and Mo'Nique push the limits of sexual discourse in the movie. Sommore begins her set complaining about her recent five-day stint in jail where lesbians continually accost her. She demands one of them to leave her alone because she has a boyfriend, and the lesbian responds, "Eatin' ain't cheatin,'" to which Sommore barks back, "Well bitch, we gonna be fightin' because I ain't dykin!" Summing up her time in jail she adds, "Baby, any place where dick ain't running free, ain't for me!" Focusing attention on her own representation, Sommore mentions that her number-one prayer is that God will give her a big ass, "cause the titties is alright but the ass is kind of flat." She remarks on how the convergence of science and medicine creates Viagra and breast implants while ignoring more important causes like Alzheimer's disease: "Do you realize that by the time we all get old, we gonna be walking around with big old titties and big old dicks and don't remember what to do with them?"

Sommore shifts to the topic of men, wishing that men would come with side-effect warnings like medicine bottles. Taking a page from Moms Mabley, she later reveals her fondness for younger men. Weary of sexing older men in dress socks who are "slipping and sliding while trying to get the pussy," she now prefers "a man with some Timberlands on, gonna be all up in that ass riding it." Sommore blames women for the fact that men with little penises are walking around thinking they got big dicks; she orders women,

"Ya'll just need to tell him the truth; shut them down!" Sommore reveals her response to her date's question about her favorite sex position: "Well, it depends on the size of the dick, cause if you got a little dick my favorite position is with another motherfucka." Like sexpert Alexyss Tylor, she offers many comments valorizing "good dick," warning women not to get dickmatized:

> You ever see somebody that's dickmatized? That's just when the dick is just too good that they just can't see the reality of some shit. People that's dickmatized be saying stupid shit like this: "No, no, no, he don't be fighting me, I be walking into the punches." That's dickmatized!

Sommore says she talks about penises a lot to even the score because female sexual anatomy is often fair game but it's not always the same with men.

> You know why I always be talking about dicks, because I believe, especially in the United States, women, we are exploited. We are. I don't give a shit which movie you want to see, *Pocahontas* or *Die Hard 3*, you are always gonna see a woman that's willing in any movie to show her pussy and her titties, so I think they should start making men show their dicks.

She declares that from now on when she pays her money for a movie she wants to see if "Wesley is Nestle"; and that for $6.50 "Denzel better swell," because this is the new millennium. She grumbles, "Fuck the bling bling! Nigga, can ya swing swing" (swinging her arm around her groin area to simulate a long penis). Similarly, a few years later in her *All New Comedy Experience* show in Chicago, Sommore explains to her audience:

> Dick don't have to be big to be good. It don't. Cause we understand as we get older it don't have to be big. . . . Men, we don't mind y'all having little dicks, we don't mind when the dick ain't big, but the only thing we say is when you don't have a big dick, don't show up with a big-dick-man's conversation. And by that I mean this: See when you have a big dick we will allow you to speak to us in a certain way. Like we allow y'all to get verbally aggressive with us—we like that shit from time to time—but when you don't have a big dick, lower your motherfuckin voice!

In an entertainment world that regularly objectifies women, Sommore employs humor about male sexual anatomy to level the playing field. By sexualizing men, female comics draw attention to the disproportionate ways men sexualize women in popular culture. Since men unabashedly treat the comic stage as safe space to sexualize every portion of a woman's body, Sommore implicitly perceives it as her feminist duty to reciprocate. Hence, Sommore's frequent references to male genitalia and sexual performance deconstruct the binaries of power regarding sexual objectification.

The last comic to hit the stage in *The Queens of Comedy* is the full-figured luminary Mo'Nique Imes, whose starring role in the syndicated sitcom *The Parkers* made her the most renowned of the bunch. Mo'Nique's specialty is to challenge Hollywood's notion of sexy by putting skinny women under ridicule. She begins her set exhorting, "Fuck you skinny bitches" to several women in the audience, before adding, "Fuck you, you skinny anorexic bulimic motherfuckers!" She proposes that skinny women are evil and need to be destroyed and summons her audience: "If you're sitting next to a skinny woman take your fist and hit that bitch on the top of her motherfuckin head!" She launches a relentless attack against a slim woman who is strolling down the aisle during her set:

> Look! Look! Skinny bitch. Look at her, look at her. See a skinny bitch is a con-
> fused bitch. It started at 10:30 bitch. You're hungry; it fucks up your thinking.
> You're gonna walk your skinny ass in during the middle of my motherfuckin
> show? Eat something.

A man stands up and waves Mo'Nique on while she chides the slim woman, prompting Mo'Nique to bark, "And sit your black ass down! Sit your country ass down!" Mo'Nique warns skinny women that they no longer should view big women as non-threatening because every man wants to "fuck a fat girl" at least one time, "and once you go fat, ya never go back!"

Mo'Nique imitates a fat woman having sex, in full control of the encounter, lifting the man up and telling him, "Hold on nigga, hold on!" After affirming the beauty and worth of big men, she admits, "I just can't fuck with you" which seems ironic when considering her preceding attack on skinny women. Yet exercising her freedom as a large woman to demand for the man to be slim is not unlike the practice of many hefty men to exclusively pursue slim and fit women. She might be unabashedly plump, but the man must meet her slim criterion. This is more than an empowering gesture in a society that constantly pressures women to conform to rigid aesthetic ideals, with men afforded the privilege of just letting themselves go.

Like Sommore, Mo'Nique engages erotic topics throughout the rest of her appearance on *The Queens of Comedy*. She offers her take on President Bill Clinton's sex scandal, arguing that oral sex is an intrinsic privilege when you are the president of the United States. She insists that if she were president she would secure oral pleasure in a similar fashion: "Line these niggas up! Your turn, your turn, your turn." She reveals that in the bedroom, her husband calls her the F.B.I.A.—Freakiest Bitch in America, because she is willing to sex him how he likes it. She lays out lurid details about the painful experience of anal sex, and after complaining about it, she adds, "But I like it now!" She presumes that every man has a little "twinkle of a bitch up in him" and instructs women on how to caress their man in a manner that "brings the bitch out of him." She tells the women to "give him a good kiss on the crack of that ass and watch that nigga break down" (and imitates the de-masculinized man). She advises women, "If you know you're gonna give your man a special treat, make sure you bathe his ass thoroughly." She positions herself and gyrates on stage to stimulate having sex doggie style, while demanding her husband to "call me a bitch, call me a bitch," which makes her feel powerful and in control. She admits that she's a "nasty filthy bitch" in the bedroom and urges women to talk that pornographic shit while they're giving it to their men.

Mo'Nique's performance in *The Queens of Comedy* as well as movie roles and reality television productions turn her into a comic legend. She is the first woman to host the fêted television program *Showtime at the Apollo*. Her bestselling book, *Skinny Women are Evil* (2004), plus her public speaking and interviews present her as a powerful woman deconstructing Hollywood notions of what it means to be beautiful and sexy. With a physical presence and personality that looms large, she is quite subversive. Her loud, crude, raunchy discourse and mannerisms defy the boundaries of what society constructs as a traditional well-behaved woman. Using humor and bombastic pronouncements in her standup, books, and interviews, Mo'Nique instructs overweight women against internalizing the oppressive mistreatment they receive from outsiders because of their size. Like Tyra Banks, Mo'Nique preaches self-love, self-awareness, and self-acceptance to women whose proportions are far beyond the boundaries of what society deems aesthetically acceptable.

Whereas thin-is-in remains the entertainment world's mantra, Mo'Nique appears brashly comfortable with her sexuality on and off stage and refuses to let her plus-size status de-sexualize her. The self-proclaimed sex symbol begins her set for the *Platinum Comedy Series* with a coterie of muscular men carrying her onto the stage, demonstrating both supreme diva status and her power to subject shirtless men to the female gaze. She is the leading lady in Anthony Hamilton's music video "Sista Big Bones" and offers her own version of Beyoncé's "Crazy in Love" dance performance on *The Soul Train Music Awards*. As host of the 2007 BET Awards, Mo'Nique dances on the stage with a group of plus-size women shaking their assets while lip-synching a song from Beyoncé's latest CD. After the seductive dance, Mo'Nique summons rapper and sex symbol L.L. Cool J. to leave the audience and come on stage for a little impromptu romantic interplay. In her guest appearance as herself on the sitcom *Girlfriends*, during her ultimate scene Mo'Nique looks in the bathroom mirror, pumps her breasts up, and congratulates herself for looking so sexy. And on her new BET nighttime talk show, you can catch Mo'Nique doing the "stripper dance" or sashaying onto the stage in sexy dresses as her co-host shouts: "Big without apology; Mo' classy, Mo' sassy!" Her star continues to rise as she wins the Oscar for Best Supporting Actress at the 2010 Academy Awards for her riveting performance as an abusive welfare mother in the critically acclaimed movie *Precious*.

Mo'Nique then has black women talking and laughing about sex in a context that men can't dominate. Her comic sets and talk show dialogues often include frank talk about her divorce, bodily functions, and sexual needs and desires. My student Emma-Caitlin puts it another way, "Mo'Nique recognizes women as human beings who fuck and fart." But Mo'Nique spends an equal amount of time balancing her sexy persona with a message of self-actualization and transcendence while exhibiting a full range of human emotions, drives, and passions. Mo'Nique's imposing physicality, brash pronouncements about sexual pleasure, and aggressive sexual imagery wield a tremendous impact on black sexual politics.

In 2009 on her BET talk show, ten years after their unprecedented tour, Mo'Nique re-assesses *The Queens of Comedy* movie as a groundbreaking achievement, "We knew we were in the midst of making history!" Mo'Nique later reunites with her three co-stars to reminisce about their experience. Sommore recalls their motives behind the movie's construction:

> At that time we were proving a point because for the longest it was said and it was known in the business that all female shows did not work. So people had never seen all females come together and do a successful show. And I think we were trying to prove to people that first of all we're women, and yes we're funny!

As the comedy queens chat about old times, the audience learns behind-the-scenes info concerning their tour, including how Sommore cruised the audiences every night to solicit male groupies. Such an admission highlights the safe space we afford to black female comics to assert their sexual agency.

While most contemporary black female comics deal with sexual topics from time to time, Sheryl Underwood takes the prize for having the raunchiest sets. She begins her *Def Comedy Jam* set in 1992 complaining about guys at the club who buy a woman a drink and then expect her to be with them all night: "That's bullshit cause two drinks might get your dick sucked but one drink ain't gonna get you shit." Sheryl prides herself as a bitch who loves to fuck more than she loves to eat, and warns the ladies in the audience that "if you let me in your house, I'll fuck your man." She admits that if you put a penis between two slices of bread you got her because "a Manwich ain't nothing but a sandwich but a dick, that's more like a meal." She commissions the men "to start eating the pussy" because her motto is, "you got to lick it before you stick it." Sheryl ends her set offering condolences to women who are with guys who refuse to pleasure them orally because: "A motherfucka ate my pussy so good up there in the dressing room that I got back in my car, drove back to Arkansas on a quarter tank of gas and slapped my mother cause that bitch didn't tell me it was that Goddamn good!" Sheryl exhorts women to orally please their men because "sucking dick make your teeth pretty."

After her *Def Comedy Jam* performance puts her on the map in the early 1990s, Sheryl continues to push the boundaries of black sexual politics with erotic routines on the road and as host of *Comic View* in the 2005-2006 season. One particular performance that appears on the *Comic View All Stars 5 DVD* begins with Sheryl raving about how sexy O.J. Simpson looks during his murder trial and then she responds to a rude male heckler in the audience, "If your pipe is about as big as your mouth, I'm gonna talk to you later!" She talks about dating fat men and points to one in the audience and says, "Yeah, I'll ride ya like Six Flags at Great America." She talks about dating a guy who is so young that he has a car phone on his big wheel, and admits to dating a handicapped guy in order to secure a better parking spot. She slams Michael Jackson for alleged sexual indiscretions, labels herself as a "retired ho," and ends her set with a surefire plan for how women can "get paid" by men:

> While you makin' love to these men and you kissin' all on them, start moving down and get all the way down, go all the way down pass the belly button. Go all the way down and right when you getting ready to go into that jungle of love, stop! That's when he's gonna say, "What's wrong, why you stop?" That's when you get paid, you say, "Damn! I forgot to pay my phone bill!"

Sheryl Underwood gives her most erotic performance to date in the *Platinum Comedy Series* in 2005. She warns Christians early on to get out the olive oil and start anointing themselves right now because her set is about to burn the place up. As usual, oral sex comes to focus as she encourages women "to suck a little more dick," and exhorts the men "to eat a smidgen of more pussy," especially on Sunday, "cause when you get your pussy sucked before going to church, don't it make you want to serve the Lord a little better?" She boldly mixes sex talk with spirituality, giving Jesus Christ a shout-out every now and then, and joking that God has a sense of humor even though she's still going to hell. This nexus of raunchy sex talk and spirituality would be offensive in any other form of public discourse, but on the comic stage, it generates pure laughter and amusement.

Sheryl's set often transgresses ethnosexual borders. She declares she'll fuck an Asian man, "cause you ain't lived until you had your pussy ate with some duck sauce on it." She asserts that a Cuban man performs oral sex on her so well that she almost goes back to Cuba with him in an inner tube. She claims that she will "fuck a white man to death," because white men will do anything to please you: "I was fuckin' this white boy; the white boy said, 'Sheryl what can I do to make you cum?' I said, 'Pay all my student loans.'" She rejects the notion that white men have small penises because when a white suitor takes off his clothes, he "started pulling out dick from everywhere" and commences "to fuck me like he hated me." While movies, television, magazines, etc. offer ample opportunities for white men to sexualize black female bodies, we see that Sheryl relegates one white sexual partner to sugar daddy status and another receives praise for his sexual prowess, demonstrating the power she wields on the comic stage to cross ethnosexual frontiers and construct male representation. By constructing white male sexual representation as potent and heavily endowed, Sheryl subversively turns the myth of black male sexual potency on its head.

Like many black female comics, Sheryl boasts about sleeping with younger men, and justifies this practice by appealing to gendered biological proclivities: "When a woman reaches her sexual peak, how old are we ladies? Thirty, forty, fifty years old. When a man reaches his sexual peak how old is he ladies? Fifteen, sixteen, seventeen years old. That's right and I will fuck a child." She adds that the only problem with sexing a young man is that he still lives at home with his momma and "I am too old to be sneakin' in a bitch's house to fuck her son on a twin bed." She then asks, "Do you know how hard it is to suck a seventeen-year-old's dick with your foot up against the door so his strong-ass mother don't bust in on you?" And when the mother finally busts in, the only thing Sheryl can say to her is, "Hey girl, didn't we go to high school together?" The irony and absurdity of her negotiating sexual space in a seventeen-year-old's twin bed while fighting off retribution from his mother, packs a serious punch into this joke. The comic stage is the rare public forum where a black woman can simulate a sexual scenario with a minor without audience offense.

Sheryl continues her highly erotic set on the *Platinum Comedy Series* with her admission that "pussy don't change no man; but a blow job will make a man reconsider his positions on a lot of shit." As a proud Republican she discusses how she loves her some President Bush, but knows he's having sex with Condoleezza Rice. She then claims she would have sucked Bill Clinton's dick, and that Monica Lewinsky didn't "know what the fuck she was doing," and asks, "How you suckin' the president's dick and you got nut stains all over your dress?" She labels Lewinsky an amateur ho, as compared to a "card-carrying, union-dues-paying, world-class federation ho" like herself who would have "sucked the skin off the president's dick and they would have never found no DNA." While taking humorous jabs at Lewinsky as well as her own lusts, she once again uses the comic stage to sexualize white men, in this case, two of the most powerful white men in contemporary American history: Bill Clinton and George W. Bush. It would be an interesting thought experiment to ponder how nineteenth-century matriarchs like Harriet Tubman or Sojourner Truth would respond to hearing a black woman sexualize two U.S. presidents. Their presumable shock would reveal Lisa Thompson's (2009) contention that we live in an unprecedented era where black women in popular culture champion sexual agency in the public sphere.

Sheryl tells a suit-wearing distinguished looking man in the audience that he comes across like the kind of guy who eats pussy with Grey Poupon. She brushes up against sexual boundaries when she tells women that "just cause you let a bitch eat your pussy don't make you gay; it makes you an opportunist." She shows solidarity with gay men: "I love gay men; any motherfucka that sucks as much dick as I do is a friend of mine, co-worker, colleague." She admits to having sex during menstruation, "cause if you men can walk through mud, you can fuck through blood. It ain't gonna kill you! It's biodegradable!" She implores men "to wash your nuts you nasty motherfuckers!" and brags that she knew she could suck a mean dick when she was six years old sitting on a corner licking an ice cream cone. She advises women to orally please their men with an Altoid in their mouth, but "don't use Halls cause when you suck a Halls down it gets thin like a razor and you can slice his dick up." She also warns women not to use the new Listermint Square to enhance fellatio because "we have not done the proper diagnostic tests at The Ho Institute to determine the exact millisecond that that Listermint Square will dissolve in your mouth. Let us finish the testing then you can use it."

Sheryl approaches the conclusion of her set with strong words for any guy who would attempt to slip drugs in her drink to take advantage of her. She claims she will outmaneuver him by reversing the glasses, allowing her to then take full sexual advantage of him:

> You're gonna wake up in my hotel room with your wrists tied with your own socks, your drawers down around your ankles. I'm gonna have you cocked over the sink like a sawed off shotgun. I'm gonna be all up in ya [she's gyrating as if she's penetrating him doggy style, presumably with a strap on] saying, "Who da man, bitch?"

Her humorous reversal depicts a man as the object of sexual invasion, for a change, placing him in a humiliating position. The comic stage offers the unexpected opportunity for a black woman to fantasize about raping and sexually humiliating a man. Her rape scenario serves the manifest function of punishing a predator, as well as the latent function of gender maneuvering by reversing the role of woman from victim to righteous avenger.

Sheryl concludes her *Platinum Comedy Series* performance by asking the women, "Wouldn't it be nice to find guys who broke our hearts in junior high school and fuck them in the ass? We'd never get caught. Ain't no man gonna tell nobody he got fucked in the ass by a girl. Could you picture him at the police station?" This joke builds on her previous mental picture of a sexual assault against a man, but this time it isn't swift retaliation against a predator, but rather a mere settling of scores with an old junior high school sweetheart. Her inimitable brand of justice demands that breaking a woman's heart deserves the punishment of rape.

While intentionally outlandish, Sheryl's male rape theme reflects her position of power on the comic stage. After the first rape fantasy, she feels too powerful to give up her position of dominance over men, so her second joke is a way of savoring that power and works on many levels. For one, the mental picture of a woman raping a man from behind is funny because it is ironic and spontaneous. Secondly, the swift justice is absurdly incompatible with her suitor's offense, which takes place way back in junior high school. Thirdly, Sheryl surmises that if the man reports her crime to the police it will bruise his manhood. So like a sly trickster, Sheryl uses the man's privileged masculinity against him to humiliate and dominate him sexually without fear of reprisal. Not many social terrains offer such ripe opportunities for this kind of creative gender maneuvering as does the comic stage.

Humor has always been a strategic device to address social issues and challenge popular culture. Comedy scholar Nancy Walker (1988) contends that feminist humor mocks gender inequality in an attempt to render it absurd and powerless. In this way, black comediennes like Sheryl Underwood are unsuspecting feminists who use wit to challenge gendered norms and sexist double standards. Female encroachment in an arena historically dominated by men, like the world of comedy, is in itself a political act.

Contemporary American men often rely on their sexual dexterity for their sense of gender identity (Seidman, Fisher, and Meeks 2006), and male comics are among the most women-objectifying, playfully misogynistic artists in popular culture. Black female comics fight fire with fire and reallocate humor as safe space to attack and objectify men. If Lynne Segal (1994) is right concerning her assumption that masculinity in Western culture depends on a particular type of sexist bravado to conceal the fact that men feel sexually vulnerable, then black female comics make men even more defenseless through candid discourse on male self-presentations and performances, acerbic commentary on male sexual incompetence, and stinging discussions about male hygiene and impotence. These comics expound on past boyfriends, good and bad sexual adventures, their own voracious sexual appetites and favorite sex positions, and fantasize about sexually assaulting men.

Academics for too long have failed to give female comics credit as feminists for using the public stage as a bully pulpit to even the score in objectifying male sexual bodies, the way men do to women in various cultural, social, and artistic environments. In a society that often consigns women to demure scripts regarding the presentation of sexual selves, black female comics bring sexual content to the forefront of public discourse. It should not surprise us, then, that the first prominent African-American woman to engage in public discourse about her same-sex spouse is Wanda Sykes, and that the location for such a subversive act is the comic stage. There are few if any public arenas outside of the comedic stage that offer black women an opportunity to brag about their skill at masturbation, announce their fantasy-cravings for minors, chastise their kids for being "cock-blockers," assess penis sizes and function, publicize sexual fantasies about powerful politicians, or chat about the vicissitudes of everyday life shared with one's same-sex spouse. It is quite possible that the next great American prophetic figure (in the vein of Martin Luther King Jr.) to attack oppressive systems of inequality, in this case sexual stratification and homophobia, is not a preacher but a black female comic.

We afford comics creative license to test the waters of offensive and shock-ing commentary because humor takes away some of the sting. Like skilled surgeons, comics anesthetize audiences with levity before proceeding to cut into them. Despite all of their excess and hyperbole, these erotic revolu-tionaries remind women of their elective power as it concerns their bodies, sexuality, and representations. Few outlets offer black women more sway to experiment with provocative discourse, more freedom to valorize sensuality, and more room to be empowered sexual subjects, than the world of standup comedy.

Chapter Nine

Tyra Banks: Erotic Talk Show Host

With my show, I wanted to create a place where women of any age could hear inspiring and moving stories that really speak to them. I hope the show gives women the feeling that they have a support system to help them deal with life—that's an empowering feeling.

—Tyra Banks

Is Tyra Banks' talk show a vehicle of female empowerment or safe space for insecure women to rage against Hollywood aesthetics? Could appearing in a bikini on the cover of a magazine ever be construed as a milestone? These questions scuttle through my brain as I watch a special episode of *The Tyra Banks Show* in 2007 honoring the ten-year anniversary of Tyra becoming the first black woman to appear exclusively on the cover of the legendary *Sports Illustrated Swimsuit Edition*. Touting it a historic event, Tyra re-shoots the cover shot in the same bikini but now ten years older and thirty pounds heavier.

As I continue to watch the show more questions surface: Is Tyra's affirmation of her new curvier figure a subversive act against the media's restrictive beauty standards, or the cry of "sour grapes" from an ex-model who rather literally no longer measures up? Does re-shooting such a photo perpetuate the objectification of women, or does such re-depiction signify Tyra as essentially controlling her representation on her own terms as an empowered subject? Is Tyra Banks a feminist? Tricky questions these are, particularly in today's postmodern age where the lines of demarcation regarding labels and distinctions seem to get dimmer and dimmer.

Thus, is Tyra Banks a feminist? After three years of analyzing one of her talk shows, I have concluded that the answer, perhaps, depends on just who possesses the privileged voice to define feminism. Tyra falls short in the eyes of many traditionalists who will label her modeling career, beauty tips, make-over sessions, and playful sexuality as politically regressive. Feminists of this ilk will also scoff at Tyra's claim that her swimsuit cover shot is an important African-American achievement. Additionally, they might rake her reality show *America's Next Top Model* over the coals for the customary cat fighting it contains along with the weekly display of women's bodies for scrutiny.

However, third-wave feminists might envision Tyra as the apotheosis of female empowerment for addressing the relevant issues affecting today's women. Traditional feminists implore women, "Value your body; ignore the male gaze." A Gen X feminist like Tyra counters, "Value your body, and don't let it go to waste!" While on one show she tells women to "develop your inner beauty and love yourselves unconditionally;" in yet another show she eagerly proclaims, "My glam squad is going to give you tips on how to maximize your body's potential." This ambivalence characterizes today's woman who often almost equally covets empowerment and style.

Tyra's appeal then is sufficient to transcend race and connect with postmodern women from various backgrounds. Many of her fans are but teenagers when Tyra emerges in *Seventeen* magazine in the late 1990s and they value her candid attention to adolescent struggles. Others learn to love their bodies and prioritize inward beauty over aesthetic appeal after reading her book *Tyra's Beauty Inside and Out*. As host of *The Tyra Banks Show*, a popular syndicated television show for the past five years, Tyra inspires millions of women, with an essential part of her impact deriving from the particular manner in which she offers her own unique brand of sexual empowerment.

From a skinny eighteen-year-old modeling in Paris, to a thirty-six-year-old talk show diva, Tyra continues to subject her body to public display. In her early twenties, her modeling agency conjures up a list of designers with the heading, "Will not book Tyra because of hips." After gaining too much weight to model high fashion, Tyra reinvents herself as a Victoria's Secret model showcasing sexy lingerie, later becoming the first African-American woman to appear on the covers of the Victoria's Secret catalogue, *GQ* magazine, and the *Sports Illustrated Swimsuit Edition*. She also dabbles with sexy movie roles in *Higher Learning* and *Coyote Ugly* along with various appearances in movies and television sitcoms. An early episode of *The Tyra Banks Show* captures her sashaying down the runway for the last time. Retiring from the walkway in 2005, Tyra becomes a media executive and host of two shows. Moreover, Tyra owns the production company that has a stake in both. In 2007, *Forbes* ranks Tyra number 62 in their list of the 100 Most Powerful Celebrities.

Tyra Banks places sexuality at the forefront of her life, message, and career as a talk show host and executive. She develops *The Tyra Banks Show* as a safe space for female lust and sexual power, which at times means relegating men to the female gaze. For example, the "Top Male Model Underwear" episode features chiseled men strutting and posing in nothing but underwear, drawing constant cheers and screams from the sexually charged female audience. Months later, Tyra brings the winner Eric back and interviews him clad in the same boxer briefs. As Eric walks onto the stage, she accosts him with a long sensual hug. There is little doubt that a curvy ex-supermodel embracing a near-nude muscular man creates an erotic moment for many people watching. Minutes later she rubs Eric's knees while seated on her studio couch before informing his father, "Daddy, I think your son is fine." Throughout the interview, she subjects Eric to intermittent touching and sexual innuendoes. This interplay reflects her fondness for controlling and objectifying male guests. It's worth noting that she is fully clothed while her male guest is almost naked during his subjection to her lustful banter. As host, Tyra is very physical and pushes the envelope of sexual suggestiveness with many of her male guests.

For another episode, Tyra goes undercover as a man and hangs out with popular hip-hop artist Chingy and his entourage. Tyra decides it would be funny and ironic to demand a kiss from Chingy while in drag. Chingy resists at first but quickly relents and lets Tyra plant a nice kiss on his lips, creating the appearance of two men kissing. Later when Tyra is back as herself interviewing Chingy, she playfully mocks him for kissing her while she was in drag. With hyper-masculinity and homophobia reigning supreme in hip-hop, Chingy's reluctance to kiss her while in drag is not surprising. Yet, Tyra's insistence provides a rare simulation of a male hip-hop star pursuing a public act of intimacy with even the illusion of another man.

On a recent episode, Tyra exposes the gendered double standard that becomes apparent when she introduces Garren James, a male prostitute, to a cheering audience. Tyra perceptively responds: "It's so funny because like if I were to have a female prostitute on the show and said she was a real-life prostitute, you guys would be like, 'ill!'" (Three years earlier, in October 2006, Tyra ventures into the secret world of illegal prostitution, and no one cheers as high-class escorts divulge intimate details about their double lives.) Following her unswerving penchant for male objectification, Tyra informs her predominantly female audience that Garren is "hung" like the television male prostitute character on the HBO television series *Hung*. On the one hand this particular episode reveals sexual stratification in that Garren, a white man swankily clad in slacks and shirt, has ample space to frame the narrative of his services more positively than media have ever conceivably allocated for female prostitutes. Tyra never preaches to Garren nor presents him as a victim, a penchant she has displayed toward female prostitutes she interviews. Hence, the show, in this case, perpetuates male sexual privilege. Yet conversely, the episode is deceptively progressive in that she does not stigmatize his female clients either, most of who are professional women. Tyra offers just as much safe space for women to justify their decision to commodify male companionship. She even sends a camera crew to follow Garren and his client Heather, a professional woman in her late twenties, on a "date," revealing the intricacies involved in negotiating services from a male escort. Heather, then, appears as a proactive independent woman acting on her on terms:

> I'm completely committed to my career and my family. I just don't have the time or the desire to be in a committed relationship. I certainly love to be around men and I miss dating but I just don't need all the drama that goes along with it. . . . It's just not my season for dating. I'm a single mom and it's really important that I focus on raising my daughter and instilling all the strong characteristics that are involved in raising a strong girl.

Millions of women watching the show expose themselves to subversive sexual scripts that provide new visions for attaining male companionship. This episode is also progressive because Tyra pokes at heteronormativity when she chides Garren, "I'm sure a lot of guys would like to hire you!" When Garren insists his services are only for women, Tyra pushes the issue by proposing: "What if a gay guy wanted to pay you $10,000 for a weekend?" At the cost of making Garren visibly uncomfortable, Tyra brings gay male lust into the conversation, negotiating on behalf of gay clients to secure his services, thus legitimizing gay sexual desires, and subverting the heterosexist assumption that only women are valid clients to commodify male companionship. Tyra's penchant for bringing LBGT issues to television discourse justifies why the Gay and Lesbian Alliance Against Defamation (GLADD) honored her with the Excellence in Media Award in 2009.

Tyra's show presents the appearance of believing the world revolves around women, and often represents men as mere trimmings to greater female concern. When men are the subject of attention, Tyra still finds a way to control and objectify their representation. For example, in one episode Tyra selects a man from the audience to be her guinea pig for the theme "the art of massaging your man." Moments later, the enthusiastic volunteer is lying shirtless on a table as Tyra receives instructions from a professional masseuse on how to work his body. Tyra runs her fingers through his hair, rubs his earlobes, and pours hot oil from a candle on his back. In a frolicsome gesture, she climbs on top of him, straddles her legs around his torso, begins pounding the man's butt with her fists, before raising her arms in victory as if she'd conquered new territory. This stranger's back and backside are now fair game for her to squeeze and punch. Tyra's playful physicality is part of her sex appeal. But sexual interplay is asymmetrical; initiating physicality with Tyra is off-limits for men, even as Tyra has perpetual license to initiate touch with them. Hence, when a man ventures on stage to be with Tyra, she is self-aware and in control.

Tyra is touchy-feely with women on her show as well. She applies moisturizer or makeup on female audience members, gives long intimate hugs, and often touches body parts of guests while giving beauty tips. At the end of a commercial clip for a future show, Tyra squeezes a woman's buttocks with both hands. Similarly, she once bumps butts with an audience member in solidarity after finding out they share the same weight.

Tyra's interview with pop vocalist Katherine McPhee provides a telling example of Tyra's playful physicality. After taking off her shoes and letting Katherine feel her corns, Tyra asks the budding star, "What's the weirdest rumor you've heard about yourself?" Katherine replies, "They're saying that my boobs are fake. It really bothers me because it's something that's ours and people are saying it's not yours." Tyra reassures her, "You have real boobs; when you walked out I saw them jiggle." Katherine agrees, "Yeah they jiggle," while gyrating to make them shake and prove her point. Tyra then asks if she can touch them. Receiving Katherine's blessing, Tyra palms the vocalist's breasts with both hands for about five seconds and then gives her a nice long hug, generating a loud laugh from the audience. After the commercial break Tyra informs her listeners, "I squeezed her boobs everybody; they are real! They are jiggly and soft." While this interplay between Tyra and her guest vocalist might seem banal or superficial to many highbrow feminist intellectuals, others may appreciate the carefree spirit and transparency.

On one show back in 2007, Tyra interviews Sasha Grey, a then eighteen-year-old adult film actress who earns almost $200,000 in her first year in the business, and who is now one of the profession's leading stars. Tyra engages this confident well-adjusted teenager in a provocative tête-à-tête, covering the topics of anal sex and Sasha's first gang-bang scene with fifteen men. Sasha shows poise and intelligence as she defends the merits of pornography as an expression of art. Although Tyra is on the more puritanical side of the discussion, her willingness to engage Sasha's world confirms her show's distinction as safe space for edgy sexual discourse.

Tyra devotes an episode to a gritty discussion about sex with a group of teenagers, discussing wild parties and oral "favors," even as their parents listen backstage. Her "Bunny Ranch" show explores the daily challenges and peculiarities of the life of legal prostitutes at a large ranch in Nevada, along with an in-depth interview with Dennis Hof, the owner of the ranch and self-professed biggest pimp in the world. As part of an undercover series, Tyra changes her name to "Chanel" and goes undercover as a stripper but panics right before her turn to deliver. Her "All About the Booty" episode discusses everything from butt implants and liposuction to butt lifts and waxing. Tyra's "Cougars on the Prowl" show features women discussing the intricacies of dating younger men and how women can develop the confidence to pursue them. Her shows hit various sides of the spectrum: one episode conducts what she dubs as America's first "Transsexual Top Model" search; while another delves into the lives of several adult guests, with ages ranging from age 24 to 39, who claim to be virgins.

Tyra has stimulating conversations with celebrity guests about sex, including former supermodel Janice Dickinson who reveals details about her sexual abuse as a child; actress Pamela Anderson who addresses the duality of being a sex symbol and mother; producer Joe Francis promoting his "Girl Gone Wild" videos; rapper and rambunctious lady's man Flavor Flav discussing his provocative reality show; Playboy mogul Hugh Hefner and his three girlfriends detailing their alternative sexual triangle; and the notorious showman former basketball star Dennis Rodman assessing his sex life with Carmen Electra and Madonna, as well as his free-spirited public displays of eroticism. In January 2008 Tyra is bold enough to ask then presidential candidate Hillary Clinton if she was embarrassed when hubby Bill had sexual relations with Monica Lewinsky. Before the senator can even formulate a carefully parsed response, Tyra belts out, "I would be embarrassed."

While her facial expressions, voice inflections, and mannerisms are often erratic and child-like, sexiness is an important part of Tyra's public persona. She frequently divulges that she loves to people-watch and fantasize about how random couples would look engaging in wild sex. Tyra endures endless interrogations concerning her dating relationships and personal relevance in pop culture, and a maelstrom of media attention concerning her alleged weight gain since retiring from the catwalk. The lion's share begins in December 2006 when Tyra is doing a photo shoot in Australia for her reality show, and a journalist takes an unflattering picture of her in a black one-piece bathing suit. By the time she comes back to the United States, the unfavorable picture appears in tabloids and across the Internet, and almost every media outlet covers the story. Tyra fights back by wearing the same one-piece on her show, and tells critics to kiss her fat ass. She also appears on the cover of *People* magazine in a hot red one-piece bathing suit and flaunts her 160-pound frame in the feature story. She continues her counterattack against Hollywood's unhealthy obsession with thinness with specially themed episodes on her talk show.

Tyra believes that women will be sexier if they maintain a positive outlook concerning their body weight and image. T-ZONE, her weeklong leadership camp for teenage girls, holds night talks about sex, dating, beauty, and body image. Similarly, her shows often discuss sexual topics, lingerie, beauty tips, weight-loss programs, and other measures to maximize one's appearance, while also addressing the perils of diseases like bulimia, anorexia, and certain kinds of plastic surgery. In makeover sessions, Tyra lets fashion experts teach women how to dress sexy and accessorize their outfits. She has a recurring segment on her show in which she or one of her guests disclose an imperfect aspect of their body and then yells "So what!" She often invites experts from *Cosmopolitan* magazine to reveal beauty and sex advice. She once goes undercover as a 350-pound woman to experience and expose the daily abuse and rejection many people face due to their weight.

On one occasion, Tyra and her entire female audience wear the same red one-piece bathing suit (like the one she sports on the *People* magazine cover), with numbers on their chests indicating their weight. A couple of weeks later Tyra and her audience are clad in sexy lingerie, exposing the contours of their bodies to millions of people. Both shows were public acts of vulnerability to encourage women to stop obsessing over their weight and to instead celebrate the female body as beautiful and sexy in all shapes and sizes. This theme is also present in her "Panty Party" show almost a year earlier when the women in the audience strip down to their bras and panties.

Tyra encourages women to be open about sex. She does an entire show about the vagina, quizzing her studio audience on its contours and complexities. A few months later she brings sex expert Sue Johanson on her show to answer questions most Americans are too shy to ask. Tyra puts her body on display as a recurring subject. A commercial advertising a forthcoming show has Tyra with her hands on her breasts saying, "My boobies! I'm going to help women put their best chest forward." On her "All About Breasts" episode she dispels rumors that her breasts are fake by having a doctor conduct a live ultrasound and various other tests to assess their naturalness.

In postmodern acts of self-reflection, Tyra presents her sexiness as a social construction, often discussing how wigs, fake eyelashes, makeup, and push-up bras help create an entirely different person on television than the Tyra her boyfriend awakes to in the morning. Tyra inspires women to be more vulnerable while also practicing what she preaches. On a recent show Tyra consoles women with these comments:

> Having been a model of over half of my life, I know a lot of people don't look like their photos. I, to this day, retouch my photos; I now have the power to be able to do that and I'll take that pen and mark it up and shave it. . . . I even started comparing myself to my own pictures, like "I don't even look like that,"

and "I'm dating this new guy, is he going to be disappointed when he sees dimples in my butt?"

On the same show Tyra reveals that she digitally retouches her calves for posters because they are thin and not in proportion to her "thick" thighs, as she describes them. While these admissions may seem to contradict her continuous pleas for women to appreciate the contours of their bodies, precisely such tension comes with the territory in a sight-and-sound media age that valorizes aesthetic perfection.

Whether it is exposing the dimples on her butt, the "cottage cheese" in the back of her thighs, the fat rolls on her back, or revealing to millions of viewers how she looks without makeup, hair-weave, and color contacts, Tyra's openness both empowers women to own their bodies and imperfections, and endorses the practice of adorning one's body with beauty accessories to enhance one's aesthetic appeal. In other words, she understands that self-acceptance is requisite for sexual satisfaction yet still strives to help women put their sexiest foot forward. Her body is an object of male fantasy, but she is also an empowered sexual subject who captivates the attention of millions of viewers each day. She teases, touches, and tantalizes as the powerful architect of her own sexual artistry. She maneuvers her sexual power and cherishes her ability to seduce those around her. Tyra fosters a setting where people are comfortable with their bodies and her physicality often generates a sexually charged environment.

All this is not to suggest that Tyra does not have her prudish moments of possibly regressive thought. In the very same episode that she presses bad boy Dennis Rodman about sexual exploits with famous women, she criticizes Karrine Steffans for publicizing her sexcapades with celebrities, which, as Karrine points out later, suggests a gendered double standard (Steffans 2007). Similarly, Tyra devotes two episodes to confronting adult film star Tyra Banxxx for using an appropriation of her name, a rather petty move for someone who made that name famous years earlier by modeling lingerie. Moreover, Tyra is on the priggish side of the discussion with Sasha Grey, assuming that the then eighteen-year-old porn star must have been a victim of sexual abuse, when in fact Sasha appears to be a confident well-adjusted woman who has since become a virtuoso performer in her profession. Apparent as they are, such prim moments nevertheless do not erase the totality of the profound ways in which Tyra exhibits an empowered sexuality.

Tyra captures the imagination of millions of fans by scratching where many twenty-first-century women are itching. She offers a hip brand of feminism that has room for complexity and contradiction: she teaches self-acceptance in one moment, and offers beauty tips on how to conceal bodily imperfections in another. She fights Hollywood's obsession with body image on one show, and advises women on how to "get the butt you've always wanted" in another show. Tyra's message for women is twofold: don't obsess over your body, but don't let it go to waste either! Her feminism is not as black-and-white as that of many preceding activists and academics. She makes it her feminist quest to broaden the constellation of women's options, hence, inspiring women to embrace complexity. But that does not make her less of a feminist than someone who is more politically active and anti-chic.

Activists and academics often forget that feminism as a movement or ideal is a social construction, which means it does not have a fixed meaning, but rather is something people interpret and reproduce to fit the needs and tastes of emerging generations. Second wave feminism is not an objective template for female empowerment, but rather a cultural product of a specific historical moment (Hollows 2000). Today's women need a new brand of feminism that resonates with the needs and tastes of today's women. Tyra has great traction with many young women who experience the gains of past women's movements as well as the requisite challenges of navigating through the matrices of a complex postmodern sight-and-sound generation. Her message of self-acceptance along with her adaptability and self-reinvention resonate with many women in our mass media age. Her transparency and vulnerability, frenetic movements, playful antics, physicality with guests, objectification of men, erotic freedom, and bold message of female empowerment push the boundaries of traditional sexual politics. Additionally, her summer leadership camp provides a context in which many African-American girls can talk openly about sex for the first time. Tyra is part of a coterie of erotic revolutionaries who insist on bringing sexual discourse to the forefront of the female experience.

Tyra Banks is also a polarizing woman who generates critics as passionate as her loyal followers. Students in my "African-American Feminist Thought" course spend an entire class period disputing her significance as an archetype of feminist empowerment. Joy feels that by teaching girls to love themselves and helping young women become confident and self-actualizing adults, Tyra is the prototypical third-wave feminist. Caroline points to the contradiction of preaching self-acceptance, while hosting a modeling show where women endure constant scrutiny based on their appearance. One student praises her courage in the midst of all her "haters," while another complains, "She is too ambitious and wants to be Oprah."

My students do find one area of consensus: they all perceive Tyra as egocentric. Well, they might have a point. Any woman who brags, "I'm starting a movement," forces guest vocalist Alicia Keyes to listen to a corny poem about how they met at Oprah's house, asks presidential candidate Barack Obama if she and her mother can have a slumber party in the Lincoln Bedroom if he's elected president, and depicts her cover story in *People* magazine as a monumental accomplishment for women's issues might be a tad egoistic. Yet is it a crime to be both courageous and self-absorbed? In our wallowing and self-indulgent culture, why should we expect our heroines to be entirely devoid of narcissism?

Curious onlookers unfamiliar with her show or career would have heard the debate and left my class wondering if Tyra is the most brave woman in the world in taking on a powerful Hollywood machine and combating negative self-image, or a scorned celebrity who rants and raves against the proverbial "pretty-girl-table" at which she once held court. Maybe the truth lies somewhere in the middle and her uncanny ability to negotiate both elements (courageous deconstruction vs. self-serving resentment) is what makes Tyra so feminist chic.

Epilogue:
Surfing the Third Wave

Feminism must be an angry, uncompromising movement that is just as insistent about our right to fuck, our right to the beauty of our individual female desires, as it is concerned with the images and structures that distort it.

—Amber Hollibaugh

As a product of the hip-hop, post-civil-rights, MTV and BET age, balancing complexity and contradiction comes as second nature for a Gen X-er like me. As such, my tastes and interests are perplexingly diverse: I listen to hip-hop and rock, Erykah Badu and Lady Gaga, Nas and Tricky. Regarding movies, I'm a zealous fan of both Woody Allen and Spike Lee. While my television preferences vary from *Girlfriends* to *The Good Wife*, I just as seamlessly read the works of feminist scholars from opposite sides of the spectrum like Patricia Hill Collins and Camille Paglia. As with my music, television, and movie tastes, I like my feminism complex, perplexingly diverse, and open to contradiction.

My own sensibilities notwithstanding, I perceive the feminist schemas of previous generations as less ambiguous. This is not to suggest that they do not have their own complexities and tensions, but rather that their agendas seem to find shape in a clearer set of objectives. Whether it is fighting for suffrage, the Equal Rights Amendment, Title IX legislation, reproductive rights, or gay and lesbian rights, objectives of the first and second waves of the feminist movement appear quite lucid when put adjacent to the murky waters that characterize my generation's feminist agendas.

I develop mixed feelings about much of the early feminist scholarship I read while carving out my feminist identity. I appreciate the battles that the second-wave women's movement launches against patriarchy, as well as its

incisive analysis of gender politics, but second wavers too often situate op-
pressors and victims in nice neat boxes. At this time I become quite familiar
with the works of Judith Butler, which dissuade me from reducing gender and
oppression to parsimonious formulas, and grow to be quite despondent with
what Gina Dent calls "missionary feminism," a dogmatic type of feminism
that "puts forward its program so stridently, guards its borders so closely, and
legislates its behavior so fervently than many are afraid to declare its name"
(1995: 64). I also begin to lose patience with a common logic in black feminist scholarship that seems to presume sex as guilty until proven innocent.

While many feminists are confrontational toward mass media, my forma-
tive years occur when women's movement ideals infiltrate music, movies,
and television, making me optimistic about popular culture. I reach my teen
years watching intelligent, successful, and charming female characters like
Jessica Fletcher and Clair Huxtable carve out new space for powerful complex women on television. Madonna and Janet Jackson show many women
from my generation that sexuality and power can go hand in hand, and The
Spice Girls infuse a sexy and adventurous kind of girl-power. I watch hip-hop
divas like Missy Elliot and Lil' Kim flaunt their sexual power. Right before
my eyes, American culture develops a new appreciation for strong athletic
women as both sexy and heroic when Madison Avenue designs commercial
campaigns with Gabrielle Reece and Marion Jones displaying new images of
female power. Hence, my childhood, teen years, and early adult years occur
in a world poles apart from my parents' generation and thus fashion me with
a different perception of female empowerment; one that often leaves me in
tension with many feminist quadrants of the past.

As I reach my mid-twenties, a series of ironies and contradictions distinguish my budding feminist identity. A month after participating in my first
"Take Back the Night" march, I read Katie Roiphe's *The Morning After*
and wonder if such marches create a climate of paranoia rather than truly
empowering women. I appear similarly ambivalent when I gripe about the
exploitation of women in hip-hop videos, and yet perceive some of their
erotic displays of black female sexuality as empowering in a crude Dionysian
sort of way. The blithe denunciation of the objectification of women by many
feminists seems warranted yet one-sided and out of beat with the cadences
of my postmodern sensibilities as an avowed complexity junkie. By the late
1990s my burgeoning feminist identity reaches a critical point.

My angst dissipates in my late twenties when I discover a so-called third
wave of feminism that emphasizes individuality and personal definitions of
feminism, while steering clear of a fixed agenda (Astrid 1994). This new
brand of feminism surfaces in the 1990s from journalists, writers, musicians,
activists, and academicians out of the raw, uncultivated vitality of younger

generations of women, making some of the deep-rooted convictions of previous feminist waves look outmoded. I identify a less dogmatic feminism in the third-wave cult classic anthology *To Be Real: Telling the Truth and Changing the Face of Feminism* and appreciate how its editor and contributors raise questions and concerns similar to those I face. During this time I also read *When Chicken Heads Come Home to Roost* by Joan Morgan, which advocates a multi-textured feminism that is brave enough to confront complexity and convinces me that younger generations must bring new experiences and raise different questions to reconstruct feminism for their ages.

My adventure into third-wave feminism exposes me to an exotic enclave of female empowerment that includes additional books like *Manifesta*, *Third Wave Agenda*, *Bulletproof Diva*, *Pin-up Grrrls*, *Swerve*, and *Built to Win*, recording artists like Ani DiFranco, angry punk rock feminists like Riot Grrls, magazines like *Bust*, and a bevy of zines and websites presenting new ways to explore feminist identity. I discover feminist sex toyshops like Toys in Babeland and Good Vibrations, the erotica of Susie Bright, and the artistic sexual communication of the Punany Poets. I discern feminist thinking styles that are conversant with "the multiple, constantly shifting bases of oppression in relation to the multiple, interpenetrating axes of identity" (Heywood and Drake 1997:3), hence blending a post-structuralist perspective with a feminist approach that also incorporates the sensibilities and perspectives of working-class feminism, black feminism, and pro-sex feminism. I engage a third-wave movement that leads women to "theorize and practice an individual feminist politics expressed more subtly in everyday-life actions" (Buszek 2006: 19) rather than a single-minded focus on organization and activism; a movement that is still global and ecological in its outlook, detests racial and sexual exclusivity, and takes a postmodernist, rather than modernist, point of reference toward art and culture, "embracing the popular and engaging with the pleasures of consumer culture" (Karlyn 2006: 55).

I soon notice that third wavers perceive women's sexual agency and exploration to be as fundamental as their right to vote. I uncover an enthralling kind of feminist who celebrates the sensual power of the geisha, nude dancer, and sexy secretary (Frank 2002), perceives her topless pose on the back cover of her novel as a demonstration of female power (Boof 2004), admits she is an avid reader of *US Weekly* and completely immersed in pop culture (Tyler 2005), challenges the forces that categorize sexual orientation (Herrup 1995), boasts that feminism makes her more proficient at sex (Valenti 2007), is curious about pornography (Walker 1995), believes a woman can work at Hooters and still be a feminist (Siegel 1997), basks in the narcissistic pleasure of beautifying herself (Senna 1995), engages in public eroticism as a form of activism (Taylor 1995), and even admits to loving hip-hop because all that in-your-face testosterone makes her nipples hard (Morgan 1999). Novelist and avowed third waver Danzy Senna explains: "This new power feminism certainly seems a sexy alternate to the 1970s party-pooping rigidity, where revolution came defined by strict dress codes" (1995: 15).

Gloria Steinem makes an important distinction between Baby Boomers who come to feminism as adults, and third wavers who "were born into a culture with many images of feminism, or they came to it young via the media and books, existing groups, and women's studies teachers, parents and siblings" (1995: xvii). Steinem underscores how feminist gains are more evident during my lifetime, even as popular culture still has more ground to cultivate concerning equitable gender representation. Whereas second wavers are more inclined to show hostility towards mass media, third wavers acknowledge that feminism in popular culture creates the starting point for successive feminist discoveries and political beliefs (Hallows and Moseley 2006). "Thus, while second wave feminists came to be understood by the media as determined to regulate sexuality, not without reason, third wave feminists rebelliously insisted on the right of consenting adults to absolute sexual freedom" (Siegel 2007: 71).

Enjoying the hard-fought rights and privileges secured by previous generations of feminist activity, third wavers typically have a different rapport with popular culture than do feminists of the past, and perhaps their boldest encroachment involves the ways they perceive sexual exploration and empowerment. Believing that the feminist elite's highbrow analysis has lost touch with the common realities of everyday women (Siegel 1997), third wavers celebrate feminist gains in popular culture, perceiving that a wide range of media representations provide suitable terrain for identity formation. Jennifer Baumgardner and Amy Richards clarify:

> The point is that the cultural and social weapons that had been identified (rightly so) in the Second Wave as instruments of oppression—women as sex objects, fascist fashion, pornographic materials—are no longer being exclusively wielded against women and are sometimes wielded by women. (2000:141)

Baumgardner and Richards contend that younger generations of women grow up during a time when celebrities like Madonna control their representation and enjoy exerting sexual power and objectifying men as a sign of strength and social standing; a time when women are not only sex objects, but also powerful sexual subjects.

In the past, popular culture often addressed female sexuality almost solely from the perspective of meeting men's needs, but in today's media landscape we see images of women as architects of their own sexual pleasure, hooking up with other women on reality shows and discussing masturbation and orgasms on television shows like *Girlfriend*s. "As third wave feminist media critics, we recognize that pop culture is a ubiquitous part of our lives" (Johnson 2007: 20), so while many feminists of the past find little promise in sexualized female images, third wavers believe that mass media have perhaps the strongest influence on shaping people's scripts of female empowerment and sexuality. Third wavers concede that many of their Gen X peers learn to connect female power with sexiness not by reading rigorous feminist tomes, but by watching television characters like Buffy the Vampire Slayer demonstrate fierce physical prowess while dressed provocatively; or pop vocalists like the Spice Girls sing about the virtues of female power while sporting low necklines and Wonder Bras (Baumgardner and Richards 2000; Karlyn 2006).

Joanne Hollows discusses a shift in scholarship from a location in which feminists situate themselves in opposition to the popular, to one in which feminists contemplate how feminism transforms the popular (2000). Feminist discussions on girl groups like the Shirelles and the Supremes (Douglas 1995), Madonna (Paglia 1992), punk rock musician Courtney Love (Heywood and Drake 1997), alternative hard rockers (Schippers 2002), pin-up girls (Buszek 2006), the *Anita Blake Vampire Hunter Series* (Siegel 2007), and television programs like *Charlie's Angels* (Womack 2003; Inness 2007), *Ally McBeal* (Hermes 2006), *Sex in the City* (Henry 2004b), *Buffy the Vampire Slayer* (Byers 2003; Siegel 2007), and *The L Word* (Moore 2007) confirm that media offer archetypes of female sexuality and empowerment.

But feminists often overlook black women when extracting archetypes of sexual empowerment from popular culture. While such an omission is partly attributable to white women enjoying more privilege in popular culture, black feminist academics who are quite conversant with black popular culture have yet to surf the third wave, and hence approach sexuality from a defensive vantage point, exemplifying contemporary black female performers as exploited sexual objects rather than as empowered subjects.

If you compose an inventory of prominent feminist scholars writing from a "pro-sex" vantage point, you will quickly notice that African Americans are conspicuously absent. Their nonappearance on such a list raises several questions: Where are the black counterparts to white scholars like Jane Gallop, Pepper Schwartz, Camille Paglia, and Katherine Frank who generate feminist theory as the driving force to advocate female sexual pleasure and agency? Why are no African-American professors writing bold and sexy feminist texts like *Erotic Faculties* by Joanna Frueh or *Pin-Up Grrrls* by Maria Elena Buszek? What does it say for the future of black sexual politics that its brightest luminaries (Patricia Hill Collins and bell hooks) are an average age of sixty? Why does third wave feminism's celebration of women's sexual pleasure and agency fail to gain traction among Gen X African-American counterparts? Perhaps the answers to the above questions lie within the politics of respectability and its rein on black feminist scholarship.

With few exceptions, black feminist thought has yet to explore the repository of sexually empowering female representations in popular culture, choosing instead to work from a substantially victimized standpoint. Instead of challenging narratives that attempt to inhibit or mute female sexual expression, black sexual politics focuses much of its energy censuring sexualized images of African-American women. Feminists swiftly categorize black women in popular culture who exude sexual energy under the stale "Jezebel" archetype without considering how some of these women subvert patriarchal scripts concerning sexual presentation and assertiveness. As a result of this myopic focus on sexual stereotyping and historic sexual objectification, sexual black women in popular culture often endure challenges to their reputations and are drenched in controversy for displaying any hint of sexual inhibition. This book hopes to strike the deathblow against the politics of respectability.

Erotic Revolutionaries: Black Women, Sexuality, and Popular Culture occupies uncharted territory in the spaces where scripting theory, third wave feminism, popular culture, and sexual politics collide. I treat cultural production and black sexual politics as strategic locations of feminist struggle. My subjects are revolutionaries who defile traditional prescriptions for female prudence, and inaugurate sexual scripts that carve new spaces for eroticism and sexual freedom. Popular culture is the battleground and sexual scripts are the weapons they deploy in a discursive war against the residual effects of male domination in society. Acknowledging that the resilience of gender regimes "depends on constantly being reinforced and reconstituted by encore gender performances" (Nagel 2003: 53), these sultry women disrupt routines of sexual stratification by providing counter-narratives against societal prescriptions that relegate proactive displays of sexuality to the male domain. Their exciting careers clash with the politics of respectability that continues to inhibit many black women from a fuller range of sexual expression.

Novelist Zane constructs fictional universes with sexually charged female protagonists. Comediennes Sheryl Underwood, Sommore, and Mo'Nique expound on past boyfriends, good and bad sexual adventures, large and small penises, irresponsible black men, as well as their own voracious sexual appetites and favorite sex positions. Internet icon Alexyss Tylor and radio personality LaDawn Black host provocative shows and write books that guide women toward protecting and celebrating the power of their sexuality. Video vixen Karrine Steffans uncovers sexual escapades with powerful celebrities, challenges gendered double standards, and promotes an adventurous image of female sexuality. Serena Williams deconstructs Victorian notions of passive femininity with her blend of strength, athleticism, and erotic power. Clergy-women Ty Adams, Juanita Bynum, and Susan Newman bring passionate sexual imagery to their sermons and writings and help women negotiate spiritual ideals with their carnal desires. Singers Janet Jackson, Jill Scott, and Beyoncé celebrate their erotic power and inspire women to be fully female and sexual. Tyra Banks designs her talk show as safe space for sexual discourse and erotic play. With their valiant and artistic displays of sexual power, black women of black popular culture have much to teach black feminists about being sexually self-aware and assertive.

By brewing a steamy gumbo of scripting theory, third wave feminism, and pop cultural representation, I hope to concoct a tastier alternative to the feminist broths we sample in pedantic consommés of academic discourse. Put more simply, I would like to contribute toward making feminism more chic. Part of the reason why feminism has such a low brand in popular circles is because media time and again portray unappealing caricatures of feminists. But a greater factor behind feminism's low brand is the fact that much feminist discourse emanates from the academic sector, a zone of society long noted for its inability to connect with the masses. You can generally count on scholars to be two things: poor marketers, and not so chic. While academics make important contributions to the theoretical mechanics of female empowerment, they also devalue the feminist brand by writing long jargon-laced tomes that only the staunchest disciples tend to read. Yes, heady theoretical works are vital for feminist progression, but so are works that address the existential needs and cultural tastes of everyday people who lack the theoretical sophistication (and patience for academic prose) to appreciate many scholarly tomes. As feminist blogger Jessica Valenti observes, "To most young women, feminism is ugly. It's unpopular. It's the anti-cool" (2007: 2). Similarly, in an interview to promote her movie Charlie's Angels, Drew Barrymore denies being a card-carrying feminist because she likes to be sexy and fun (Womack 2003). Someone should inform Barrymore that feminism is all about empowering women to be sexy and fun.

Aware of my own limitations as a scholar, I employ artistic and proactive women of popular culture to articulate a more chic vision of female empowerment. For example, when a celebrity like Aisha Tyler proudly proclaims she is a feminist and admonishes women to stop fearing the f-word, she gives the feminist brand a sexy upgrade from the caricature of grouchy women in scratchy wool suits. But more importantly, when she writes about feminism and sexual politics, academics can learn new strategies concerning how to package feminist empowerment. Tyler exploits the art of the misdirect by writing a humorous and sexy book that packs a feminist sucker punch; she makes women laugh while she expands their consciousness with subversive scripts. In her book *Swerve*, she constructs an image of a bad-ass, sassy, pedicure-loving, joke-telling, sexy-on-her-own-terms kind of feminist that is definitely more chic than what most academics have to offer in terms of feminist archetypes. If pop cultural figures like Tyler are acquainted with nothing else, they know how to be sexy and fun, which is something academics can exploit to raise the chic levels on the feminism thermometer. My blend of scripting theory and pop cultural representation serves toward this end of making feminism theoretical, sexy, and chic.

Susan Douglas (1995) demonstrates, more than any other academic, the strategic nexus between feminism and popular culture, displaying how media play important roles in raising women's consciousness. Douglas suggests that when a woman goes off to college, takes women's studies courses, and concomitantly declares herself a feminist her choice is not a decisive leap from unconscious to conscious because popular culture has been prepping her toward feminist awareness since her youth. Hence, one way to infuse flamboyance and style into feminism is to follow Douglas's lead and accentuate the ways in which popular culture offers up subversive sexual scripts that endorse female empowerment. *Erotic Revolutionaries* demonstrates how scholars can form a symbiosis between feminist theorizing and pop cultural representation to offer people a more proactive vision of female sexuality. Hopefully this work will inspire more academics to do the same and use black women in popular culture as archetypes of female empowerment rather than solely referencing the cases in which they are exploited victims.

Jeffrey Weeks (1985) confirms that a small number of topics induce as much angst and pleasure, anguish and hope, dialogue and quiet as the erotic potential of our bodies. I anticipate this work will persuade many feminists to employ the analytically rich sociological framework of scripting theory, a social constructionist model that conceptualizes sexuality as an imminently social phenomenon, explores the social and historical context that shapes sexuality, and emphasizes sexualities as products of discourses, rather than of nature or biological forces. I also believe this book will inspire a conceptual ménage à trois between black sexual politics, scripting theory, and third wave feminism. As scholars from all three camps develop a greater fondness for each other's monumental contributions toward imagining new visions of female empowerment, they can extract much about sexuality from powerful black women in popular culture who are dismantling politics of silence, deconstructing gendered double standards on sexuality, and demolishing sexual expectations that deny women a full range of sexual expressivities. The erotic revolutionaries discussed in this book offer a unique style of activism and should arouse more feminist scholarship to engage black women in pop culture from an offensive position.

We are at a crucial time in history, a post-paradigmatic era when there is no all-encompassing worldview, social structure, or grand narrative that constitutes human behavior. Our society is more fragmented than ever before; manifold meanings, competing visions for human life and society are prevalent. The multiple sourcing of knowledge transmission through media mechanisms like cable television, satellite radio, the Internet, self-publishing, etc. makes this an exciting time to be alive, a time of change and contestation, a strategic era to launch counter-narratives against oppressive regimes, and hence a great time to articulate new visions for gender dynamics and sexuality. Popular culture has never been more disjointed and hence never riper for intellectual integration. Feminists must ferret through these manifold messages for narratives that lead us toward a more equitable humanity.

The erotic revolutionaries discussed in this book are products of this postmodern era of change and their appeal in the marketplace lends much to our understanding of the discursive powers of media to provide multiple narratives to help people negotiate the complex realities of social life and individual identity. Scripting theory provides us with a remarkably handy metaphor toward understanding how such negotiation takes place. In this way this book is prescriptive and apologetic. It is not an objective discussion of the social construction of sexuality, but rather a polemic against discursive strategies that hold black women to conservative sexual standards. Too often the feminist rage against the perceived objection of black female bodies is fueled by bourgeois values that shun most sexual expressivities. Black sexual politics must surf the third wave and reject the politics of respectability by accentuating sexual agency, pleasure, and empowerment.

References

Adams, Ty. 2006. *Single, Saved, and Having Sex*. New York and Boston: Warner Books.

Baldwin, James. 2000. *Go Tell It on the Mountain*. New York: Dial Press.

Banks, Ingrid. 2000. *Hair Matters: Beauty, Power, and Black Women's Consciousness*. New York and London: New York University Press.

Barres, Pamela Des. 2005. *I'm With the Band: Confessions of a Groupie*. Chicago: Chicago Review Press.

Battle, Juan, and Sandra L. Barnes. Introduction. In *Black Sexualities: Probing Powers, Passions, Practices, and Politics*, eds. Juan Battle and Sandra L. Barnes, 1-12. New Brunswick, NJ: Rutgers University Press.

Baumgardner, Jennifer, and Amy Richards. 2000. *Manifesta: Young Women, Feminism, and the Future*. New York: Farrar, Straus and Giroux.

Black, LaDawn. 2007. *Let's Get It On: 15 Hot Tips and Tricks to Spice up Your Sex Life*. New York: One World Books.

Billingsley, ReShonda Tate. 2007. *The Pastor's Wife*. New York: Pocket Books.

Bobo, Jacqueline. 1995. Black Women as Cultural Readers. New York: Columbia University Press.

Boof, Kola. 2004. *Flesh and the Devil*. Hemet Mountain, CA: Door of Kush.

Bordo, Susan. 1993. *Unbearable Weight: Feminism, Western Culture and the Body*. Berkeley: University of California Press.

Bowen, Michele. 2005. *Church Folk*. West Bloomfield, MI: Walk Worthy Press.

Boyd, Julia. 1997. *Embracing the Fire: Sisters Talk about Sex and Relationships*. New York: Dutton.

Brown, Lyn Mikel. 2003. *Girlfighting: Betrayal and Rejection among Girls*. New York and London: New York University Press.

Bryan, Carmen. 2007. *It's No Secret: From Nas to Jay-Z, from Seduction to Scandal —A Hip-Hop Helen of Troy Tells All*. New York: VH1 Books.

Bryant, Niobia. 2006. *Heated*. New York: Kensington.

Buszek, Maria Elena. 2006. *Pin-up Grrrls: Feminism, Sexuality, Popular Culture.* Durham and London: Duke University Press.

Butler, Judith. 1990. *Gender Trouble: Feminism and the Subversion of Identity.* New York and London: Routledge.

———. 1993. *Bodies That Matter: On the Discursive Limits of "Sex."* New York and London: Routledge.

Byers, Michelle. 2003. "Buffy the Vampire Slayer: The Next Generation of Television." In *Catching a Wave: Reclaiming Feminism for the 21ˢᵗ Century*, eds. Rory Dicker and Alison Piepmeier, 171-187. Boston: Northeastern University Press.

Cahn, Susan K. 1993. "From the 'Muscle Moll' to the 'Butch' Ballplayer: Manishness, Lesbianism, and Homophobia in U.S. Women's Sports." In *Feminist Studies* 19: 343-361.

———. 1994. *Coming on Strong: Gender and Sexuality in Twentieth-Century Women's Sports.* New York: The Free Press.

Cannon, Katie Geneva. 1995. *Katie's Canon: Womanism and the Soul of the Black Community.* New York: Continuum.

———. 2004. "Sexing Black Women: Liberation from the Prisonhouse of Anatomical Authority." In *Loving the Body: Black Religious Studies and the Erotic*, eds. Anthony B. Pinn and Dwight Hopkins, 11-30. New York: Palgrave Macmillan.

Carby, Hazel. 1999. *Cultures in Babylon: Black Britain and African America.* London and New York: Verso.

Chambers, Veronica. 1996. *Mama's Girl.* New York: Riverhead Books.

Collins, Patricia Hill. 2004. *Black Sexual Politics: African Americans, Gender, and the New Racism.* New York and London: Routledge.

———. 2006. *From Black Power to Hip-hop: Racism, Nationalism, and Feminism.* Philadelphia: Temple University Press.

Daly, Meg. 2000. "The Allure of the One-Night Stand." In *Sex and Single Girls: Straight and Queer Women on Sexuality*, ed. Lee Damsky, 194-204. Seattle: Seal Press.

Davis, Angela. 1981. *Women, Race, and Class.* New York: Random House.

———. 1999. *Blues Legacies and Black Feminism: Gertrude "Ma" Rainey, Bessie Smith, and Billie Holliday.* New York: Vintage.

Denfeld, Rene. 1995. *The New Victorians: A Young Woman's Challenge to the Old Feminist Order.* New York: Warner Books.

———. 1997. *Kill the Body, the Head Will Fall: A Closer Look at Women, Violence, and Aggression.* New York: Warner Books.

Dent, Gina. 1995. "Missionary Position." In *To Be Real: Telling the Truth and Changing the Face of Feminism*, ed. Rebecca Walker, 61-75. New York and London: Anchor Books.

Dickinson, Janice. 2002. *No Lifeguard on Duty: The Accidental Life of the World's First Supermodel.* New York: Harperentertainment.

Dines, Gail, Robert Jensen, and Ann Russo. 1998. *Pornography: The Production and Consumption of Equality.* New York: Routledge.

Douglas, Kelly Brown. 1999. *Sexuality and the Black Church*: A Womanist Perspective. Maryknoll, NY: Orbis Books

Douglas, Susan. 1995. *Where the Girls Are: Growing Up Female with the Mass Media*. New York: Three Rivers Press.

Dow, Bonnie. 1996. *Prime-Time Feminism: Television, Media Culture, and the Women's Movement Since 1970*. Philadelphia: University of Pennsylvania Press.

Dworkin, Andrea. 1991. *Pornography: Men Possessing Women*. New York: Plume.

Dworkin, Shari. 2007. " 'It's Less Work for Us and It Shows Us She Has Good Taste': Masculinity, Sexual Initiation, and Contemporary Sexual Scripts." In *The Sexual Self: The Construction of Sexual Scripts*, ed. Michael Kimmel, 105-121. Nashville: Vanderbilt University Press.

Edmondson, Jacqueline. 2005. *Venus and Serena Williams: A Biography*. Westport CT: Greenwood Press.

Epstein, Steven. 2007. "The Badlands of Desire: Sex Research, Cultural Scenarios, and the Politics of Knowledge Production." In *The Sexual Self: The Construction of Sexual Scripts*, ed. Michael Kimmel, 249-263. Nashville: Vanderbilt University Press.

Escoffier, Jeffrey. 2004. "Foreword." In *An Interpretation of Desire: Essays in the Study of Sexuality*, by John Gagnon, xii-xxvi. Chicago and London: University of Chicago Press.

Fisher, Nancy. 2006. "Purity and Pollution: Sex as a Moral Discourse." In *Introducing the New Sexuality Studies: Original Essays and Interviews,* eds. Steven Seidman, Nancy Fisher, and Chet Meeks, 51-58. London and New York: Routledge.

Fonda, Jane. 2006. *My Life So Far*. New York: Random House.

Foucault, Michel. [1976] 1980. *The History of Sexuality Volume 1: An Introduction*. New York: Vintage Books.

Frank, Katherine. 2002. "Stripping, Starving, and the Politics of Ambiguous Pleasure." In *Jane Sexes It Up: True Confessions of Feminist Desire*, ed. Merri Lisa Johnson, 171-206. New York and London: Four Walls Eight Windows.

Frederick, Marla. 2003. *Between Sundays: Black Women and Everyday Struggles of Faith*. Berkeley and Los Angeles: University of California Press.

Frueh, Joanna. 1997. *Erotic Faculties*. Berkeley: University of California Press.

Frug, Mary Joe. 2000. "The Politics of Postmodern Feminism: Lessons from the Anti-Pornography Campaign." In *Feminism & Pornography*, ed. Drucilla Cornell, 254-263. Oxford and New York: Oxford University Press.

Gagnon, John. 2004. *An Interpretation of Desire: Essays in the Study of Sexuality*. Chicago and London: University of Chicago Press.

Gagnon, John, and William Simon. 1973. *Sexual Conduct: The Social Sources of Human Sexuality*. Chicago: Aldine Publishing Company.

Gallop, Jane. 1997. *Feminist Accused of Sexual Harassment*. Durham and London: Duke University Press.

Gamson, Joshua. 2006. "Popular Culture Constructs Sexuality: Interview with Joshua Gamson." In *Introducing the New Sexuality Studies: Original Essays and Interviews,* eds. Steven Seidman, Nancy Fisher, and Chet Meeks, 337-341. London and New York: Routledge.

Gilbert, Joanne. 2004. *Performing Marginality: Humor, Gender, and Cultural Critique*. Detroit: Wayne State University Press.

Godfrey, Phoebe Christina. 2006. "Law and the Regulation of the Obscene." In *Introducing the New Sexuality Studies: Original Essays and Interviews,* eds. Steven Seidman, Nancy Fisher, and Chet Meeks, 349-356. London and New York: Routledge.

Goffman, Erving. 1959. *The Presentation of Self in Everyday Life.* New York: Anchor Books.

Gomez, Jewelle. 1993. *Forty-Three Septembers: Essays by Jewelle Gomez.* Ithaca NY: Firebrand Books.

Gottschild, Brenda Dixon. 2003. *The Black Dancing Body: A Geography from Coon to Cool.* New York: Palgrave Macmillan.

Greer, Germaine. 1971. *The Female Eunuch.* New York: McGraw-Hill.

Guilbert, Georges-Claude. 2002. *Madonna as Postmodern Myth: How One Star's Self- Construction Rewrites Sex, Gender, Hollywood, and the American Dream.* London: McFarland and Co.

Haggins, Bambi. *Laughing Mad: The Black Comic Persona in Post-Soul America.* New Brunswick, NJ, and London: Rutgers University Press.

Hammonds, Evelynn. 1994. "Black (W)holes and the Geometry of Black Female Sexuality." *Differences: A Journal of Cultural Studies* 6: 126-145.

———. 1999. "Toward a Genealogy of Black Female Sexuality: The Problematic of Silence." In *Feminist Theory and the Body: A Reader*, eds. Janet Price, 93-104. New York: Routledge.

Henry, Astrid. 2004. *Not My Mother's Sister: Generational Conflict and Third-Wave Feminism.* Bloomington: Indiana University Press.

———. 2004b. "Orgasms and Empowerment: Sex and the City and the Third Wave Feminism." In *Reading Sex and the City*, eds. Kim Akass and Janet McCabe, 65-82. London and New York: I.B. Tauris.

Hermes, Joke. 2006. " 'Ally McBeal', 'Sex and the City' and the Tragic Success of Feminism." In *Feminism in Popular Culture*, eds. Joanne Hollows and Rachel Moseley, 79-96. New York and Oxford: Berg.

Herrup, Mocha Jean. 1995. "Virtual Identity." In *To Be Real: Telling the Truth and Changing the Face of Feminism*, ed. Rebecca Walker, 239-251. New York and London: Anchor Books.

Heywood, Leslie. 2000. "All-American Girls: Jock Chic, Body Image and Sports." In *Body Outlaws: Young Women Write about Body Image and Identity*, ed. Ophira Edut, 201-210. Emeryville, CA: Seal Press.

Heywood, Leslie, and Jennifer Drake. 1997. *Third Wave Agenda: Being Feminist, Doing Feminism.* Minneapolis: University of Minnesota Press.

Heywood, Leslie, and Shari Dworkin. 2003. *Built to Win: The Female Athlete as Cultural Icon.* Minneapolis and London: University of Minnesota Press.

Higginbotham, Evelyn Brooks. 1992. "African-American Women's History and the Meta Language of Race." *Signs* 17: 251-274.

Hine, Darlene Clark. 1989. "Rape and the Inner Lives of Black Women in the Middle West." *Signs* 14: 912-920.

Hollibaugh, Amber. 1996. "Desire for the Future: Radical Hope in Passion and Pleasure." In *Feminism and Sexuality: A Reader*, eds. Stevi Jackson and Sue Scott, 1-31. New York: Columbia University Press.

Hollows, Joanne. 2000. *Feminism, Femininity and Popular Culture*. Manchester and New York: Manchester University Press.

Hollows, Joanne, and Rachel Moseley. 2006. "Popularity Contests: The Meanings of Popular Feminism." In *Feminism in Popular Culture*, eds. Joanne Hollows and Rachel Moseley, 1-22. Oxford and New York: Berg.

Holmberg, Carl B. 1998. *Sexualities and Popular Culture*. Thousand Oaks, CA: Sage Publications.

hooks, bell. 1981. *Ain't I a Woman: Black Women and Feminism*. Boston: South End Press.

———. 1990. *Yearning: Race, Gender, and Cultural Politics*. Cambridge, MA: South End Press.

———. 1992. *Black Looks: Race and Representation*. Cambridge, MA: South End Press

———. 1996. *Reel to Real: Race Sex and Class at the Movies*. New York and London: Routledge.

———. 2000. *Feminist Theory: From Margin to Center*. Cambridge, MA: South End Press.

Hunter, Heather. 2007. *Insatiable: The Rise of a Porn Star*. New York: St. Martin's Press.

Hutcherson, Hilda. 2002. *What Your Mother Never Told You About Sex*. New York: G.P. Putnam's Sons.

———. 2006. *Pleasure: A Woman's Guide to Getting the Sex You Want, Need, and Deserve*. New York: Perigee Books.

Imes, Mo'Nique. 2004. *Skinny Women Are Evil: Notes of a Big Girl in a Small-Minded World*. New York: Atria.

Inness, Sherrie. 2007. "Introduction: Who Remembers Sabrina? Intelligence, Gender, and the Media. In Geek Chic: Smart Women in Popular Culture, ed. Sherrie Inness, 1-10. New York: Palgrave Macmillan.

Jackson, Stevi. 2007. "The Sexual Self in Late Modernity." In *The Sexual Self: The Construction of Sexual Scripts*, ed. Michael Kimmel, 3-15. Nashville: Vanderbilt University Press.

Jackson, Stevi, and Sue Scott. 1996. "Sexual Skirmishes and Feminist Factions: Twenty- Five Years of Debate on Women and Sexuality." In *Feminism and Sexuality: A Reader*, eds. Stevi Jackson and Sue Scott, 1-31. New York: Columbia University Press.

James, Joy. 1999. *Shadowboxing: Representations of Black Feminist Politics*. New York: St. Martin's Press.

James, Kelly. 2006. "Sexual Pleasure." In *Introducing the New Sexuality Studies: Original Essays and Interviews*, eds. Steven Seidman, Nancy Fisher, and Chet Meeks, 45-50. London and New York: Routledge.

Jenkins, Candice. 2007. *Private Lives, Proper Relations: Regulating Black Intimacy*. Minnesota and London: University of Minnesota Press.

Johnson, Kalyn, Tracey Lewis, Karla Lightfoot, and Ginger Wilson. 2001. *The BAP Handbook: The Official Guide to the Black American Princess*. New York: Broadway Books.

Johnson, Merri Lisa. 2002a. "Jane Hocus, Jane Focus: An Introduction." In *Jane Sexes It Up: True Confessions of Feminist Desire*, ed. Merri Lisa Johnson, 1-11. New York and London: Four Walls Eight Windows.

———. 2002b. "Fuck You & Your Untouchable Face: Third Wave Feminism & the Problem of Romance." In *Jane Sexes It Up: True Confessions of Feminist Desire*, ed. Merri Lisa Johnson, 13-50. New York and London: Four Walls Eight Windows.

———. 2007. "Ladies Love Your Box: The Rhetoric of Pleasure and Danger in Feminist Television Studies." In *Third Wave Feminism and Television: Jane Puts It in a Box*, ed. Merri Lisa Johnson, 1-27. London and New York: I.B. Tauris.

Jones, Lisa. 1994. Bulletproof Diva: Tales of Race, Sex, and Hair. New York: Doubleday.

Karlyn, Kathleen Rowe. 2006. "Feminism in the Classroom: Teaching Towards the Third Wave." In *Feminism in Popular Culture*, eds. Joanne Hollows and Rachel Moseley, 57-75. New York and Oxford: Berg.

Kelis. 2005. "Selling Sexuality." In *Naked: Black Women Bare all About Their Skin, Hair, Hips, Lips, and Other Parts*, eds. Ayana Byrd and Akiba Solomon, 101- 104. New York: The Berkley Publishing Group.

Kimmel, Michael. 2007. "John Gagnon and the Sexual Self." In *The Sexual Self: The Construction of Sexual Scripts*, ed. Michael Kimmel, vii-xix. Nashville: Vanderbilt University Press.

Knowles, Tina. 2002. *Destiny's Style: Bootylicious Fashion, Beauty, and Lifestyle Secrets from Destiny's Child*. New York: Harper Entertainment.

Koedt, Anne. 1972. *Radical Feminism*. New York: Quadrangle.

Kuhn, Thomas. 1996. *The Structure of Scientific Revolutions*. Chicago: University of Chicago Press.

Laumann, Edward O., Jenna Mahay, and Yoosik Youm. 2007. "Sex, Intimacy, and Family Life in the United States." In *The Sexual Self: The Construction of Sexual Scripts*, ed. Michael Kimmel, 165-190. Nashville: Vanderbilt University Press.

Laumann, Edward O., John H. Gagnon, Robert T. Michael, and Stuart Michaels. 2000. *The Social Organization of Sexuality: Sexual Practices in the United States*. Chicago: University of Chicago Press.

Lavin, Susan. 2004. *Women and Comedy in Solo Performance: Phyllis Diller, Lily Tomlin, and Roseanne*. New York and London: Routledge.

Lorde, Audre. 1984. *Sister Outsider: Essays and Speeches by Audre Lorde*. Berkeley and Toronto: Crossing Press.

Luke, Renee. 2006. *Making Him Want It*. New York: Kensington.

MacKinnon, Catharine A. 1989. *Toward a Feminist Theory of the State*. Cambridge: Harvard University Press.

———. 1996. *Only Words*. Cambridge: Harvard University Press.

McLaren, Margaret. 2002. *Feminism, Foucault, and Embodied Subjectivity*. Albany, NY: State University of New York Press.

Millett, Kate. 1970. *Sexual Politics*. New York: Doubleday.

"Miss T." 2006. *The Guide to Becoming the Sensuous Black Woman: And Drive Your Man Wild in and out of Bed!* Philadelphia: Oshun Publishing.

Moore, Candace. 2007. "Getting Wet: The Heteroflexibility of Showtime's The L Word." In *Third Wave Feminism and Television: Jane Puts It in a Box*, ed. Merri Lisa Johnson, 119-146. New York: I.B. Tauris.

Morgan, Joan. 1999. *When Chickenheads Come Home to Roost: A Hip-Hop Feminist Breaks It Down*. New York: Simon and Schuster.

Murray, Victoria Christopher. 2005. *Temptation*. West Bloomfield, MI: Walk Worthy Press.

Nagel, Joane. 2003. *Race, Ethnicity, and Sexuality: Intimate Intersections, Forbidden Frontiers*. New York and Oxford: Oxford University Press.

Naija. 2006. *Between My Thighs: An Urban Erotic Tale*. New York: Brown Erotic Publishing.

Neal, Mark Anthony. 2003. *Songs in the Key of Black Life: A Rhythm and Blues Nation*. New York and London.

Nelson, Jill. 2005. *Sexual Healing: A Novel*. New York: Pocket Books.

Newman, Susan. 2002. *OH GOD!: A Black Woman's Guide to Sex and Spirituality*. New York: One World Books.

Noire. 2006. *G-Spot: An Urban Erotic Tale*. New York: One World/Ballantine.

Paglia, Camille. 1992. *Sex, Art, and American Culture: Essays*. New York: Vintage Books.

Plante, Rebecca. 2007. "In Search of Sexual Subjectivities: Exploring the Sociological Construction of Sexual Selves." In *The Sexual Self: The Construction of Sexual Scripts*, ed. Michael Kimmel, 31-48. Nashville: Vanderbilt University Press.

———. 1994. *Vamps and Tramps: New Essays*. New York: Vintage Books.

Plummer, Ken. 2007. "Queers, Bodies, and Postmodern Sexualities: A Note on Revisiting the 'Sexual' in Symbolic Interactionism." In *The Sexual Self: The Construction of Sexual Scripts*, ed. Michael Kimmel, 16-30. Nashville: Vanderbilt University Press.

Pough, Gwendolyn. 2004. *Check It While I Wreck It: Black Womanhood, Hip-Hop Culture, and the Public Sphere*. Boston: Northeastern University Press.

Raines, Jenyne. 2003. *Beautylicious!: The Black Girl's Guide to the Fabulous Life*. New York: Harlem Moon.

Reed, Jennifer. 1997. "Roseanne: A 'Killer Bitch' for Generation X." In *Third Wave Agenda: Being Feminist, Doing Feminism*, eds. Leslie Heywood and Jennifer Drake, 122-133. Minneapolis: University of Minnesota Press.

Riggs, Marcia. 2003. *Plenty Good Room: Women versus Male Power in the Black Church*. Cleveland: Pilgrim Press.

Roberts, Tara. 1997. *Am I the Last Virgin?: Ten African American Reflections on Sex and Love*. New York: Simon and Schuster.

———. 2007. *What Your Mama Never Told You: True Stories about Sex and Love*. Boston: Graphia.

Robinson, Patricia Murphy. 1992. "The Historical Repression of Women's Sexuality." In *Pleasure and Danger: Exploring Female Sexuality*, ed. Carole S. Vance, 251-266. London: Pandora Press.

Roby, Kimberla Lawson. 2002. *Casting the First Stone*. New York: Kensington.

———. 2005a. *Too Much of a Good Thing*. New York: Avon Books.

———. 2005b. *The Best-Kept Secret*. New York: Avon Books.

Roiphe, Katie. 1994. *The Morning After: Sex, Fear, and Feminism*. Bel Air, CA: Back Bay Books.

Rose, Tricia. 1994. *Black Noise: Rap Music and Black Culture in Contemporary America*. Middletown, CT: Wesleyan University Press.

———. 2003. *Longing to Tell: Black Women Talk about Sexuality and Intimacy*. New York: Farrar, Straus and Giroux.

Ross, Alex. 2007. *The Rest Is Noise: Listening to the Twentieth Century*. New York: Farrar, Straus, and Giroux.

Rowe-Finkbeiner, Kristin. 2007. *The F-Word: Feminism in Jeopardy—Women, Politics and the Future*. Berkeley, CA: Seal Press.

Rubin, Gayle. 1992. "Thinking Sex: Notes for a Radical Theory of the Politics of Sexuality." In *Pleasure and Danger: Exploring Female Sexuality*, ed. Carole S. Vance, 267-319. London: Pandora Press.

Schippers, Mimi. 2002. *Rockin' Out of the Box: Gender Maneuvering in Alternative Hard Rock*. New Brunswick, NJ, and London: Rutgers University Press.

Schwartz, Pepper, and Virginia Rutter. 1998. *The Gender of Sexuality*. Thousand Oaks, CA: Pine Forge Press.

Scott, Jill. 2008. *The Moments, the Minutes, the Hours: The Poetry of Jill Scott*. New York: St. Martin's Griffin.

Segal, Lynne. 1994. *Straight Sex: Rethinking the Politics of Pleasure*. Berkeley and Los Angeles: University of California Press.

Seidman, Steven, Nancy Fisher, and Chet Meeks. 2006. *Introducing the New Sexuality Studies: Original Essays and Interviews*. London and New York: Routledge.

Senna, Danzy. 1995. "To Be Real." In *To Be Real: Telling the Truth and Changing the Face of Feminism*, ed. Rebecca Walker, 5-20. New York and London: Anchor Books.

Sharpley-Whiting, T. Denean. 2007. *Pimps Up, Ho's Down: Hip-hop's Hold on Young Black Women*. New York and London: New York University Press.

Shockley, Ann Allen. 1987. *Say Jesus and Come to Me*. Tallahassee, FL: The Naiad Press.

Siegel, Carol. 2007. "Female Heterosexual Sadism: The Final Feminist Taboo in Buffy The Vampire Slayer and the Anita Blake Vampire Hunter Series." In *Third Wave Feminism and Television: Jane Puts It in a Box*, ed. Merri Lisa Johnson, 56-90. New York: I.B. Tauris.

Siegel, Deborah. 1997. "Reading Between the Waves: Feminist Historiography in a 'Post Feminist' Moment." In *Third Wave Agenda: Being Feminist, Doing Feminism*, eds. Leslie Heywood and Jennifer Drake, 55-82. Minneapolis: University of Minnesota Press.

Simon, William. 1996. *Postmodern Sexualities*. London and New York: Routledge.

Simon, William, and John Gagnon. 1984. "Sexual Scripts." *Society* 22:53-60.

———. 2003. "Sexual Scripts: Origins, Influences and Changes." *Qualitative Sociology* 26: 491-497.

Simson, Rennie. 1983. "The Afro-American Female: The Historical Context of the Construction of Sexual Identity." In *Powers of Desire: The Politics of Sexuality*, eds. Ann Snitow, Christine Stansell, and Sharon Thompson, 229-235. New York: Monthly Review Press.

Souljah, Sister. 1994. *No Disrespect*. New York: Vintage Books.

Staples, Robert. 2006. *Exploring Black Sexuality*. Lanham, Maryland: Rowman and Littlefield.

Steffans, Karrine. 2005. *Confessions of a Video Vixen*. New York: Amistad.

———. 2007. *The Vixen Diaries*. New York and Boston: Grand Central Publishing.

Steinem, Gloria. 1995. "Forward." In *To Be Real: Telling the Truth and Changing the Face of Feminism*, ed. Rebecca Walker, xiii-xxviii. New York and London: Anchor Books.

Tanenbaum, Leora. 2000. *Slut!: Growing Up Female with a Bad Reputation*. New York: HarperCollins.

Tasker, Yvonne. 1993. *Spectacular Bodies: Gender, Genre and the Action Cinema*. New York: Routledge.

Tatum, Stephanie. 2009. "Black Female Sex Workers: Racial Identity, Black Feminist Consciousness, and Acculturated Stress." In *Black Sexualities: Probing Powers, Passions, Practices, and Politics*, eds. Juan Battle and Sandra L. Barnes, 311-326. New Brunswick, NJ: Rutgers University Press.

Taylor, Jocelyn. 1995. "Testimony of a Naked Woman." In *To Be Real: Telling the Truth and Changing the Face of Feminism*, ed. Rebecca Walker, 219-237. New York and London: Anchor Books.

Thompson, Lisa B. 2009. *Beyond the Black Lady: Sexuality and the New African American Middle Class*. Urbana and Chicago: University of Illinois Press.

Tiefer, Leonore. 1995. *Sex Is Not a Natural Act and Other Essays*. Boulder, CO: Westview Press.

———. 2007. "Sexuopharmacology: A Fateful New Element in Sexual Scripts." In *The Sexual Self: The Construction of Sexual Scripts*, ed. Michael Kimmel, 239-248. Nashville: Vanderbilt University Press.

Turner, Tina, with Kurt Loder. 1986. *I, Tina: My Life Story*. New York: Avon Books.

Tyler, Aisha. 2005. *Swerve: Reckless Observations of a Postmodern Girl*. New York: Plume.

Ussher, Jane M. 1997. *Fantasies of Femininity: Reframing the Boundaries of Sex*. New Brunswick, NJ: Rutgers University Press.

Valenti, Jessica. 2007. *Full Frontal Feminism: A Young Woman's Guide to Why Feminism Matters*. Berkeley: Seal Press.

Vance, Carole S. 1992. "Pleasure and Danger: Toward a Politics of Sexuality." In *Pleasure and Danger: Exploring Female Sexuality*, ed. Carole S. Vance, 1-27. London: Pandora Press.

Waldby, Catherine. 1995. "Destruction: Boundary Erotics and Reconfigurations of the Heterosexual Male Body." In *Sexy Bodies: The Strange Carnalities of Feminism*, eds. Elizabeth Grosz and Elspeth Probyn, 266-277. London: Routledge.

Walker, Nancy. 1988. *A Very Serious Thing: Women's Humor and American Culture*. Minneapolis: University of Minnesota Press.

Walker, Rebecca. 1995. "Being Real: An Introduction." In *To Be Real: Telling the Truth and Changing the Face of Feminism*, ed. Rebecca Walker, xxix-xxxix. New York and London: Anchor Books.

Wallace, Michele. 1990. Invisibility Blues: From Pop to Theory. London and New York: 1990.

Walter, Natasha. 1998. *The New Feminism*. London: Little, Brown & Company.

Weeks, Jeffrey. 1985. *Sexuality and Its Discontents: Meanings, Myths, and Modern Sexualities*. London: Routledge and Kegan Paul.

———. 2006. "The Social Construction of Sexuality: Interview with Jeffrey Weeks." In *Introducing the New Sexuality Studies: Original Essays and Interviews*, eds. Steven Seidman, Nancy Fisher, and Chet Meeks, 14-20. London and New York: Routledge.

West, Cornel. 1999. "On Black Sexuality." In *The Cornel West Reader*, ed. Cornel West, 514-520. New York: Basic Civitas.

West, Traci C. 2004. "A Space for Faith, Sexual Desire, and Ethical Black Ministerial Practices." In *Loving the Body: Black Religious Studies and the Erotic*, eds. Anthony B. Pinn and Dwight Hopkins, 31-50. New York: Palgrave Macmillan.

Williams, Elsie. 1995. *The Humor of Jackie Moms Mabley: An African American Comedic Tradition*. New York and London: Garland Publishing.

Williams, Linda. *Hard Core: Power, Pleasure, and the Frenzy of the Visible*. Berkeley: University of California Press.

Williams, Venus, and Serena Williams. 2005. *Serving from the Hip: Ten Rules for Living, Loving, and Winning*. Boston: Houghton Mifflin Company.

Womack, Whitney. 2003. "Reevaluating 'Jiggle TV': Charlie's Angels at Twenty-Five." In *Disco Divas: Women and Popular Culture in the 1970s*, ed. Sherrie A. Inness, 151-171. Philadelphia: University of Pennsylvania Press.

Wurtzel, Elizabeth. 1998. *Bitch: In Praise of Difficult Women*. New York: Doubleday.

Wyatt, Gail. 1997. *Stolen Legacy: Reclaiming Our Sexuality, Taking Back Our Lives*. Hoboken NJ: Wiley.

Wyatt, Gail and Lewis Wyatt. 2003. *No More Clueless Sex: 10 Secrets to a Sex Life That Works for Both of You*. Hoboken NJ: Wiley.

Zane. 1998. *Addicted*. New York and London: Atria Books.

———. 2000. *The Sex Chronicles: Shattering the Myth*. New York and London: Atria Books.

———. 2001. *Shame on It All*. New York and London: Atria Books.

———. 2002a. *Gettin' Buck Wild: Sex Chronicles II*. New York and London: Atria Books.

———. 2002b. *The Heat Seekers*. New York: Downtown Press.

———. 2003a. *Nervous: A Novel*. New York and London: Atria Books.

———. 2003b. *The Sisters of APF: The Indoctrination of Soror Ride Dick*. New York and London: Atria Books.

———. 2003c. *Skyscraper: A Novel*. New York and London: Atria Books.

———. 2005. *Afterburn: A Novel*. New York and London: Atria Books.

———. 2007. *Dear G-Spot: Straight Talk about Sex and Love*. New York and London: Atria Books.

———. 2009. Head Bangers: An APF Sexcapade. Largo, MD: Strebor Books.

Index

About the Author

Shayne Lee has quickly emerged as one of the leading interpreters of contemporary American culture, providing commentary in the *New York Times*, *USA Today, Washington Post*, *Atlantic Monthly*, and various other periodicals, as well as through numerous appearances on radio and television. Lee received a PhD in Sociology from Northwestern University and is now Associate Professor of Sociology and African Diaspora Studies at Tulane University. Lee is also the author of *T.D. Jakes: America's New Preacher* and co-author of *Holy Mavericks: Evangelical Innovators and the Spiritual Marketplace*, both published by New York University Press.